Wheatland Bounty

by
The Laboratory Technologists
of Saskatchewan

Wheatland Bounty

by
The Laboratory Technologists of Sask.

ISBN 0-9690753-0-8

1st Printing — May, 1981, 5,000 copies
2nd Printing – August, 1981, 5000 copies
3rd Printing – December, 1981, 10,000 copies
4th Printing – April, 1983, 10,000 copies
5th Printing – November, 1987, 5,000 copies
6th Printing – December, 1988, 5,000 copies
7th Printing – December 1990, 5,000 copies
8th Printing – March 1999, 5,000 copies

Copyright © 1981
by the Saskatchewan Branch of
The Canadian Society of Laboratory
Technologists. All rights reserved.

The Saskatchewan Branch of the C.S.L.T.
P.O. Box 3837
Regina, S4P 3R8
Saskatchewan, Canada

Designed, Printed, Produced and Distributed in Canada by
Centax Books/Publishing Solutions/PrintWest Group
Publishing Director: Margo Embury
1150 Eighth Avenue, Regina, Saskatchewan, Canada S4R 1C9
Telephone: (306) 525-2304 FAX: (306) 757-2439

Publishing a cookbook of this quality and standard is a mammoth undertaking, as you can well appreciate. This book was compiled and organized by a small group of medical technologists in Saskatchewan.

The idea was introduced quite simply in the initial planning steps for the 1982 National Congress of the Canadian Society of Laboratory Technologists, to be hosted by the Regina academy. We said to ourselves, and then to our colleagues, wouldn't it be exciting to gather a collection of favorite recipes from the 1000 technologists in Saskatchewan? The idea grew, and excitement spread from city to city, then town to country. From the initial communication onwards, the co-operation and enthusiasm of hundreds of people has been unified and heart-warming.

Then the work began! A committee of ten Regina ladies convened and set in motion the wheels of organization. Recipes were collected and sorted, typed and tested, with the invaluable aid of many volunteers. Every recipe submitted came from the homes of Saskatchewan technologists and their forebearers! Each recipe chosen to be contained in this prized collection was double tested by the committee members and their co-workers. For this purpose, the Regina academy hosted pot luck suppers and bake sales, in addition to all the personal evaluations. Thus we are able to claim with pride and confidence that this printing is tried and true! We are assured that the success and credibility of this book will be reflected in your kitchen, and in the compliments from your friends and family.

The committee has worked diligently and devotedly towards a common goal — the production of a masterpiece! The purpose of the project was initially to provide financial aid towards the Congress, and the provincial Society, for management and educational use. However, we now envision many public and social benefits to medical technology in general. Perhaps, as the success of this book spreads, so will the awareness and understanding of thousands of families towards medical technology as an exacting and vital career.

We hope that as you use this book, you will think of us as a group of dedicated individuals, who work and believe conscientiously in the co-operation amongst the health teams. Our career is both challenging and stimulating, with demands as great as the achievements. Similarly, this project has proven challenging and rewarding; thus in many ways, the parallel with our work life is evident. The standards and quality of our training are necessarily very high, ensuring the skill and reliability of each individual. Likewise, we have maintained rigid standards and high quality in the production of our cookbook, so that each individual creation is reminiscent of our beliefs.

Thus, I would like to personally thank each of my committee members and friends who have worked with me so hard, thus enabling the project to proceed smoothly and efficiently. I am proud to have been able to co-ordinate this publication into a manual to be enjoyed by so many, so often.

On behalf of all the medical technologists in Saskatchewan, I wish you happiness and success with this cookbook. We were thinking of you as we put each page together, so perhaps you will think of us as you turn them.

Sincerely,

Christina Patoine

Chairman
Cookbook Committee

Pride is something I'm not short of these days.

First, I'm proud to be a medical technologist. It's an exciting, stimulating career — and this cookbook endeavor has made it even more so!

Secondly, I'm proud to be able to make a contribution as a cook. I think everyone pretends to be a gourmet cook, and this gave us a chance to exhibit and develop our culinary abilities.

Thirdly, I'm proud to be a part of the organization of a National Congress. The proof is in the pudding, success of the sale of this book will reflect the success of our '82 Congress.

Proudly,

Georgia Hearn

Chairman,
1982 Congress Committee

Tasty Treats Within

Party Pleasers	Page 9
Soups & Salads	Page 29
Garden Greats	Page 55
Casserole Concoctions	Page 71
Marvellous Meats	Page 91
Sweet Tooth Successes	Page 135
Flour Power	Page 191
Canning & Condiments	Page 225
Metric Conversions	Page 239
Simple Substitutions	Page 240
Household Hints	Page 241
Index	Page 245

Party Pleasers

**BEVERAGES
APPETIZERS
SNACKS**

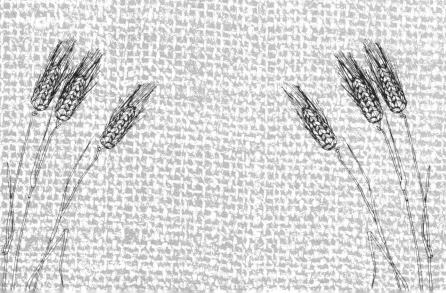

Wedding Punch

- 2 12½ ounce cans frozen orange juice
- 2 12½ ounce cans frozen pink lemonade
- 3 25 ounce bottles gingerale
- 1 26 ounce bottle Crackling Rose wine
- 1 26 ounce bottle gin or vodka
- ¼ bottle (6½ ounces) Southern Comfort

slices of lemons and oranges
ice cubes

In a punch bowl combine orange juice, lemonade, gingerale, wine and gin or vodka. Add Southern Comfort. Gently mix in slices of oranges and lemons and ice cubes. Serve with a smile. *You could substitute an ice-wreath for the ice cubes. To make wreath: just place lemon and orange slices, maraschino cherries, mint leaves, etc. in the base of a doughnut shaped jelly mold. Add water to a depth of about 2 inches. Freeze. Just before serving, remove ice wreath from mold and place in punch, fruit side up. This adds a festive visual appeal.*

Yields 184 ounces or 46 4 ounce servings.

Aleatha Schoonover, Saskatoon

Beer Punch

- juice of 4 lemons, or ½ cup
- ¾ cups white sugar
- 2 15 ounce cartons frozen raspberries or strawberries
- 2 12 ounce bottles 7-Up
- 12 bottles cold beer

Mix lemon juice and sugar until the sugar dissolves. Add fruit and mash with a fork. Add 7-Up and beer.

Makes about 35 to 40 6 ounce drinks.

Lynn Smith, Regina

Summer Joy Punch

- 1   15 ounce box frozen strawberries
- 1   orange rind, chopped
- 3   6 ounce cans frozen lemonade
- 9   6 ounce cans water
- 1   25 ounce bottle gingerale
- 1   26 ounce bottle vodka (optional)

Mix in a punch bowl the strawberries, orange rind, lemonade, water, gingerale and vodka. Orange slices may be added to punch bowl for decoration.

Yields 30 4 ounce punch cup servings.

Elaine Kurtz, Regina

Banana Slush

- 6   cups water
- 1   cup sugar
- 2   6 ounce cans frozen lemon juice
- 2   6 ounce cans frozen orange juice
- 5   mashed bananas
- 1   48 ounce can unsweetened pineapple juice

gingerale

Boil sugar and water and cool. Add frozen juices and bananas that have been put in the blender. Add pineapple juice and mix.

Freeze in plastic gallon pail stirring periodically until frozen.

You could also add Vodka, gin or other liquor.

Serve with gingerale or 7-Up. *Makes a good cool summer drink.*

Yields 160 ounces or 40 4 ounce drinks.

Karen Kenway, Nipawin

Hawaiian Slush

1	48 ounce can unsweetened pineapple juice	6	ounces water
3	6 ounce cans frozen pink lemonade	5	ounces lime cordial
		1	26 ounce bottle vodka (optional)
			gingerale

Mix together the juices, water, lime cordial and vodka, if used. Put the mixture into an ice cream pail and freeze. To serve, put about 3 ounces slush into a glass and fill with chilled gingerale.

Yields 35 3 ounce servings of slush.

Emily Lett, Regina

Frozen Dacquiri

1	25 ounce bottle liquid dacquiri mix	1	26 ounce bottle white rum
2	12 ounce cans frozen limeade	2	25 ounce bottles 7-Up
2	12 ounce cans water	1	cup icing sugar

Combine all ingredients. Divide mixture into 3 2-quart containers (or several smaller containers), and place in the freezer. Stir the mixture once or twice a day until crystalline through. Serve from an ice bucket.

Yields 150 ounces.

Laurel Madole, Regina

Winter Warmers

Coffee

½ ounce Maple liqueur
½ ounce brandy
1 mug of coffee
2 tablespoons whipped cream
2 tablespoons Kahlua

In the mug add the liqueur, brandy and coffee. Top with the whipped cream and drizzle the Kahlua over this.

Tea

1 cup tea
1 ounce Amaretto (almond liqueur)

Mix liqueur and tea together and serve in a brandy snifter.

Hot Chocolate

1 ounce Swiss Chocolate almond liqueur
1 mug hot chocolate
2 tablespoons Amaretto

Mix the Swiss chocolate liqueur and the hot chocolate together. Top with the Amaretto liqueur. *Great ways to come in from the cold!*

Linda Taylor, Melville

Honey Bunch Punch

1   48 ounce can pineapple-grapefruit drink, chilled
1¼ cups orange juice, chilled
1   26 ounce bottle soda water, chilled

Combine ingredients. Serve over ice. Makes 14 6 ounce servings.

Eileen Woodham, Regina

Russian Tea

2   3¼ ounce packages
    Lemon crystals (juice)
4   3¼ ounce packages
    orange crystals (juice)
½   cup instant tea
    (powdered)

1½ cups sugar (optional)
1   teaspoon cinnamon
½   teaspoon ground cloves

Mix all ingredients together well and store in a jar or cannister. Add 1½ or 2 teaspoons to a mug and pour in hot water. *Has a spicy apple flavour.*

Eileen Woodham, Regina
Linda Tidball, Regina
Astrid Hoogendoorn, Regina

Carob Drink

4   cups cold milk
1   tablespoon carob powder
½   teaspoon vanilla

½   teaspoon cinnamon
2   tablespoons honey

Mix milk, flavorings and honey together in a blender until frothy. The drink can be served cold or can be heated up like hot chocolate. If desired a banana can be added to replace the honey.

Joanne Sorenson, Glaslyn

Wassail

6 cups apple juice or cider	1 18 ounce can unsweetened pineapple juice
1 cinnamon stick	
¼ teaspoon nutmeg	
¼ cup honey	cinnamon sticks
3 tablespoons lemon juice	
1 teaspoon grated lemon peel	

In large saucepan, heat apple juice and one cinnamon stick to boiling; reduce heat. Cover, simmer 5 minutes. Uncover, stir in nutmeg, honey, lemon juice, lemon peel, pineapple juice and simmer 5 minutes longer. Serve in punch bowl. Use cinnamon sticks as individual stirrers. Makes 16 servings, about ½ cup each. *A good hot drink that both adults and children enjoy, especially in the winter.*

Judy Jones, Regina

Eggnog Brasilia

4 eggs, separated	½ cup light corn syrup
3 cups milk	½ cup white rum
2 cups light cream	¼ cup water
3 tablespoons instant coffee	ground nutmeg

Beat egg yolks slightly in a large saucepan; stir in milk, cream, coffee and ¼ cup of the syrup. Heat slowly, stirring constantly, until scalding. Remove from heat and stir in the rum. Heat the remaining ¼ cup of the syrup with the water to boiling in a small pan. Simmer 5 minutes. Beat egg whites till foamy in a large bowl, then slowly beat in hot syrup until meringue forms soft peaks. Fold in eggnog mixture. Pour eggnog into a punch bowl, and sprinkle with nutmeg. Serve warm. Makes 24 punch cup servings.

Christina Patoine, Regina

Easy Eggnog

½ cup sugar
3 egg yolks
¼ teaspoon salt
4 cups scalded milk
3 egg whites

⅛ teaspoon salt
¼ cup sugar
vanilla
nutmeg
cinnamon (to taste)

Beat ½ cup sugar, egg yolks and salt. Stir in scalded milk slowly. Cook, stirring constantly till mixture coats the spoon. Cool. Beat egg whites, salt, remaining sugar, vanilla and spices and add to the custard. Mix thoroughly. Chill, for 4 hours. *Delicious!*

Linda Taylor, Melville

Festive Punch

2½ cups pineapple juice
1 quart lime sherbet
1 quart vanilla ice cream
1 25 ounce 7-Up

1 25 ounce gingerale
1 26 ounce bottle of vodka (optional)

Melt the sherbet and ice cream in advance by leaving it in the fridge overnight.

Combine all ingredients in the punch bowl. Mix well.

Yields 160 ounces or 40 4 ounce servings.

Laurel Madole, Regina

Recipe For A Good Lab Tech

500 mls knowledge
500 mls patience
250 mls common sense
250 mls self-confidence
  50 mls alertness
  50 mls helpfulness
  50 mls humour

Measure knowledge, patience and common sense accurately into a large beaker; blend well. Fold in self-confidence.

In a test tube place alertness and helpfulness; vortex well before titrating with humour.

Place these two mixtures together in a well-equipped lab. This recipe keeps for a long time if properly preserved!

Smoked Salmon Spread

1	8 ounce package cream cheese	1	teaspoon liquid smoke
2	tablespoons finely grated onion	¼	teaspoon salt
		½	cup chopped walnuts
1	tablespoon lemon juice	2	tablespoons parsley
1	tablespoon horseradish	2	cups canned salmon, drained

Soften cream cheese. Add onion, lemon juice, horseradish, liquid smoke, walnuts and seasonings. Mix well. Add the salmon and mix again. *Chill overnight, for the best flavor, before serving with a variety of crisp crackers.*

Frances Walker, Regina

Olive 'n' Cheese Rolls

1	cup shredded Cheddar cheese	½	teaspoon salt
¼	cup soft butter	⅛	teaspoon paprika
½	cup all-purpose flour	24	to 28 pimento stuffed olives

Blend cheese and butter. Sift flour, salt, and paprika and blend into cheese mixture. Work into a ball and roll out onto a sheet of wax paper to about ¼ inch thickness. Cut in ½ inch strips. Roll each olive in a strip of cheese dough. Bake on an ungreased baking sheet in a 350°F. oven for 15 minutes.

Ham slices rolled up may be substituted for the olives, or any dill pickles, or gherkins, if desired. *You can count on compliments when your guests taste these tangy appetizers.*

Doreen Chomicki, North Battleford

Shrimp, Ham or Mushroom Hors D'Oeurves

1	8 ounce package cream cheese, softened	3	tablespoons margarine
½	cup soft margarine	1	teaspoon salt (omit when using ham)
½	cup flour	¼	teaspoon pepper
		¼	teaspoon thyme
1	10 ounce can mushrooms, drained, or 1 6 ounce can shrimp, drained, or ½ pound of canned ham, diced	2	tablespoons flour
		¼	to ½ cup sour cream
		1	or 2 eggs, beaten
1	medium onion, finely chopped		

Dough:

Beat together the cream cheese, margarine and ½ cup of flour to form a dough. Do not over beat. Refrigerate 1 hour.

Filling:

Fry together the mushrooms, or shrimp or ham, with the onion and margarine. Stir in the spices and sour cream, to which the flour has been added. Heat gently.

Roll out the dough thinly and cut 2 inch to 3 inch circles. Put 1 tablespoon of the stuffing on each circle, fold over and pinch edges. Brush edges with beaten egg and prick with a fork. Bake on a cookie sheet at 400°F. to 450°F. for 15 minutes.

Julia Westerman, Fort Qu'Appelle

Hot Meat and Cheese Puffs

1	pound hamburger	1	pound sharp Cheddar cheese, shredded
1	teaspoon salt		
1	teaspoon pepper	3	cups biscuit baking mix
1	teaspoon oregano	¾	cup water
1	teaspoon paprika		

Brown meat with spices added. Drain off fat and cool completely. In a large bowl mix shredded cheese, cooled meat and biscuit mix. Add water and mix with a fork until just blended. With greased hands roll into 1 inch balls. Bake on cookie sheets in 400°F. oven for 12 to 15 minutes or until puffed and brown. *Serve plenty of these hot snacks, they will be a real favorite. May be frozen for later use. Cool completely and freeze in plastic bags. Reheat when still frozen at 375F° for 10 minutes.*

Frances Walker, Regina

Pickled Shrimp and Mushrooms

¼	cup lemon juice	¼	teaspoon mustard powder
2	tablespoons vinegar		
⅛	cup salad oil	2	medium onions, grated
¼	teaspoon salt	1	4 ounce can shrimp, drained and rinsed
dash of pepper			
1	clove garlic, minced	1	10 ounce can whole mushrooms, drained
1	bay leaf		

To make the marinade, combine the lemon juice, vinegar, oil, seasonings and onions. Then add the shrimp and mushrooms. Let stand refrigerated for 24 hours in a covered jar.

Marilyn Elmer, Saskatoon
Holly Hastie, Regina

Shrimp Cheese Ball

2	8 ounce packages cream cheese	1	green onion, chopped fine
1	4 ounce can shrimp, drained and rinsed	2	teaspoons butter
¼	of a 5 ounce can oysters (rinsed with water if oil packed ones are used)	½	teaspoon parsley
		½	teaspoon tarragon
			dash of seasoned salt
½	stalk celery, chopped fine	1	small package bacon or barbeque flavored potato chips

Cream the cheese. Add minced shrimp and oysters. Add celery, onions, butter and seasonings. Form mixture into a ball and roll in the crushed potato chips to coat. Place in refrigerator for at least an hour. *Serve with crackers and olives.*

Nona Burrows, Central Butte

Cheese Walnut Log

3	ounces cream cheese	1	tablespoon lemon juice
2	cups shredded old Cheddar cheese	¼	teaspoon garlic powder
1	pound Herb and Spice cheese		crushed walnuts for garnish

Bring cheeses to room temperature. Combine cheeses, lemon juice and garlic powder and mix till fluffy. Shape into a log. Roll in walnuts. Chill 4 to 6 hours.

Joy Sanders, Humboldt

Curry Dip

½ cup mayonnaise
½ cup plain yogurt
½ to 1 teaspoon curry powder
½ teaspoon turmeric
¼ teaspoon chili powder
¼ teaspoon ginger
¼ teaspoon paprika
salt to taste

Mix all ingredients together. Refrigerate at least 1 hour before serving. *To serve, place bowl of curry dip in the center of a large tray and arrange crisp raw vegetables around it.*

Lennie Pruden, Nipawin

Vegetable Dip

1 cup sour cream or plain yogurt
1 cup salad dressing
1 tablespoon minced onion flakes
1 tablespoon dill weed
1 tablespoon parsley flakes
½ tablespoon garlic powder

Mix all ingredients together. Let stand in refrigerator for 2 hours. *Serve with a variety of fresh vegetables.*

Debra Dumontel, Regina

Bacon Wrapped Water Chestnuts

1	8 ounce can water chestnuts, drained	¼	cup soya sauce
8	slices bacon, cut in half	½	teaspoon ground ginger
		½	teaspoon garlic salt

Wrap each water chestnut in half slice of bacon. Secure with a toothpick.

Combine remaining ingredients. Pour over the bacon-chestnuts. Refrigerate overnight or several hours, basting sauce over the chestnuts from time to time.

Drain. Place on rack in baking dish. Broil, turning frequently, until bacon is cooked.

Microwave: Cover with a paper towel. Cook 2 minutes, turn dish and cook 2 to 4 minutes longer until bacon is done.

Joan Brash, Regina

Crab Dip

1	8 ounce package cream cheese	1	teaspoon horseradish
1	tablespoon milk	1	6 ounce can flaked crab meat, drained
1	tablespoon finely chopped onion		salt and pepper to taste
1	shake of Worcestershire sauce		slivered almonds to garnish

Mix milk and onion with the creamed cheese. Add flavorings and crab meat, and mix well. Put in a shallow dish, and sprinkle with slivered almonds. Bake at 375°F. until hot.

Jacquie Fauth, Regina

Chili Con Queso Dip

1	19 ounce can tomatoes, drained thoroughly	1	5 ounce can chillies, chopped
1	pound Velveeta cheese, finely cubed	1	tablespoon dried onion
			tortilla chips

Chop the tomatoes. Add cheese, chillies and onion. Heat until cheese melts and dip is bubbling hot. *Serve with tortilla chips.*

Jean Schropp, Regina

Shrimp Dip

1	10 ounce can tomato soup	2	7 ounce cans small shrimp, drained
3	12 ounce packages cream cheese	2	tablespoons plain gelatin (optional)
1	cup salad dressing	½	cup cold water (optional)
1	cup finely chopped celery		
½	cup finely chopped onions		

Bring tomato soup to a gentle boil. Add cream cheese and mix thoroughly to melt. Remove from heat.

Add salad dressing, celery, onions and shrimp. Pour mixture into lightly greased mold(s). Chill.

For firmer molds, add the gelatin softened in cold water just before pouring into the mold. *Serve shrimp dip with fresh, cut up vegetables or crackers or potato chips.*

Laureen Cuddington, Prince Albert

Fresh Fruit Dip

1 cup sour cream
2 tablespoons icing sugar
2 teaspoons mint
¼ teaspoon cardomon, crushed

Mix ingredients in a blender.

Delicious as a dip for chunks of cantaloupe, honeydew melon, strawberries, avocado, pineapple, etc.

Kathy Keller, Regina

Bacon Dip 'n' Dunk

10 slices bacon, chopped
1 cup plain yogurt
¼ cup mayonnaise or salad dressing
1 tablespoon finely chopped green onion
1 tablespoon finely chopped parsley
½ teaspoon seasoned salt

Cook the bacon until crisp. Drain well, and set aside.

Reserve 1 tablespoon of the bacon drippings and combine with the yogurt and mayonnaise. Add onion, parsley and seasoned salt. Crumble the bacon, and add to yogurt mixture. Mix well.

Cover and refrigerate for several hours to blend flavors. *This makes a great dip for chips, crackers or fresh vegetables.*

Georgia Hearn, Regina

Christmas "Kutia"

This is a traditional Ukrainian Christmas Eve dish.

1	cup wheat		pinch of salt
6	cups water	½	cup chopped nuts
½	cup poppy seeds	½	cup chopped apples, unpeeled (optional)
1	cup white sugar or honey		
1	cup boiling water		

Pick out all the foreign objects from the wheat. Wash and place in a heavy pot. Add the water and soak overnight.

In the morning, do not drain, but bring the wheat to a boil and skim the scum off the top. Turn to low heat, cover and simmer for 4 to 5 hours or until kernels burst open. Stir occasionally while it is cooking, to prevent sticking.

Wash the poppy seeds well in a fine cloth. Scald and simmer for about 5 minutes. Drain well in a cheese cloth.

Add the poppy seeds to the wheat. Mix the sugar or honey, and salt in the boiling water, and stir into the wheat mixture. Cool, then refrigerate. Add nuts and apples, if used, before serving. This can be served either warm or chilled.

Instead of simmering the wheat on the stove top, it may also be cooked overnight in a slowcooker, on low.

Evelyn Hull, Willowbrook
Doreen Chomicki, North Battleford

Toasted Granola

½	cup salad oil	½	cup sesame seeds
½	cup honey	½	cup wheat germ
5	cups rolled oats, or a mixture of rolled grains (wheat, rice, triticale)	½	cup bran
		1	cup medium coconut
		1	cup raisins
1	cup sunflower seeds, unsalted	1	cup almonds or other nuts

Heat oil and honey until well mixed. Mix together the rolled oats, sunflower seeds, sesame seeds, wheat germ and bran. Pour the honey mixture over top and toss well to coat. Place on a cookie sheet and bake at 250°F. for 20 to 25 minutes, or until toasted, stirring often.

Remove from the oven and add the coconut, raisins and almonds or other nuts. Return to oven for another 5 minutes.

Mary Woodsworth, Saskatoon
Judy Jones, Regina

Cheese Snack

½ pound white Monteray Jack or Cheddar cheese

Preheat oven to 350°F. Grease a baking sheet well. Cut cheese into ½ inch cubes and space about 3 inches apart on baking sheet. Bake for 7 minutes or until edges become light brown. Watch carefully; the fat will cook out of the cheese, leaving little spaces, to give the effect of lace. Store in airtight container.

Makes 3½ to 4 dozen.

Judy Jones, Regina

Soups & Salads

**SOUPS
CHOWDERS
SALADS**

Fruit — Marshmallow Salad

18¾ ounce can crushed pineapple	1 ripe banana, sliced
⅔ cup uncooked rice	1 cup whipping cream
⅔ cup water	2 tablespoons chopped marachino cherries or 2 tablespoons fruit cocktail
½ teaspoon salt	
2 teaspoons lemon juice	
1½ cups miniature marshmallows	

Drain the can of pineapple and save juice. Combine the rice, water, pineapple juice and salt. Stir to moisten. Bring to boil, cover and simmer 15 minutes, or until rice is soft. Remove from heat, let stand 5 minutes. Add pineapple and lemon juice. Cool. Stir in the miniature marshmallows and banana. Whip the whipping cream until stiff. Fold the whipped cream and the cherries (or fruit cocktail) into the rice mixture. Chill thoroughly.

Serves 8.

Karen Pearce, Regina

Macaroni Salad

4 cups raw macaroni	½ cup chopped green onion
½ cup Catalina French dressing	½ cup chopped celery
2 cups grated carrots	2 6 ounce cans drained broken shrimp
1 cup grated cabbage	1½ cups mayonnaise

Cook macaroni as directed on box. Drain, cover with hot water and drain well again. Coat macaroni with dressing and cool.

Rinse the drained shrimp well in cold water. Add the vegetables, shrimp and mayonnaise to the macaroni, mixing well. Let stand at least 12 hours in refrigerator. *This will keep up to a week in the refrigerator.*

Anna Clark, Moose Jaw

14 Day Coleslaw
"Of Cabbages and Kings..."

1 medium large head cabbage, finely shredded
2 medium large carrots, finely shredded
1 white onion, grated
1 or 2 green peppers, shredded

Dressing:

1½ cups vinegar
½ cup water
1½ cups white sugar
1½ teaspoons salt
1 teaspoon celery seed
1½ teaspoons mustard seed
½ teaspoon turmeric (optional, it colors salad yellow)

Combine salad vegetables in a large bowl.

To make dressing, mix together vinegar, water, sugar and salt. Put celery seed and mustard seed in a cheesecloth bag; add to vinegar mixture. Bring to a boil, making sure that the sugar is dissolved. Remove cheesecloth bag, and cool thoroughly.

Pour cooled dressing over all vegetables. Mix well. Let stand 12 hours in refrigerator before using. *This coleslaw keeps well for 14 days. It is crisp and never softens. Keep it in a jar in your refrigerator, ready to serve. Excellent for lunch boxes, and picnics.*

Yields about 12 servings.

Pearl Fahlman, Fillmore
Joyce Sloan, Regina
Beverly Creusot, Regina
Carole Coulthard, Regina
Iva Cameron, Swift Current
Shirley Gillander, Regina
Audrey Thibodeau, Regina

Sauerkraut Salad

1	32 ounce jar sauerkraut, drained	1	medium green pepper chopped
2	medium onions chopped	1	cup white sugar
½	cup pimento chopped	½	cup salad oil
1	cup celery chopped fine	½	cup cider vinegar

Mix vegetables together in a large bowl. Mix sugar, oil, vinegar and bring to a boil. Pour hot liquid over mixed vegetables. *This will keep indefinitely.*

Sheila Toeckes, Shaunavon

Cool Chicken Salad

1	cup cold, chopped cooked chicken	¼	cup chopped dill pickle
1	cup shredded lettuce	2	chopped hard boiled eggs
⅓	cup chopped green pepper	2	tablespoons salad oil
¼	cup chopped green onions	1	heaping tablespoon mayonnaise
½	cup chopped zucchini, unpeeled		salt and pepper to taste

Toss together the chicken, vegetables, and eggs in a salad bowl.

Mix the oil and mayonnaise to make the dressing, and add to the salad just before serving. Salt and pepper to taste. *This makes a nice, fresh luncheon for 2 or 3 people. It can be prepared the day before, except for adding the dressing, thus can be a time saver, too.*

Christina Patoine, Regina

Marinated Carrot Salad

2   pounds carrots, sliced in circles
1   large spanish onion, thinly sliced in rings
1   large green pepper, sliced in strips
1   10 ounce can tomato soup
1   cup white sugar
½   cup cooking oil
¾   cup vinegar
1   teaspoon salt
1   teaspoon black pepper

Cook carrots until tender-crisp and drain. Add onions and green pepper and set aside.

Combine the soup, sugar, oil, vinegar and seasonings in a small pot. Boil, stirring to dissolve the sugar. Pour over the vegetables and cook on low heat for 2 to 4 minutes.

If desired, pack in sterilized jars and seal. Cool and store in the fridge. Allow to marinate at least overnight before using.

Alternately, the marinated vegetables may be removed from the dressing with a slotted spoon and served over lettuce.

This makes approximately 4 pint jars.

Sharon Zimmer, Regina
Anita Veikle, Cut Knife
Pat Mialkowsky, Saskatoon
Lois Miller, Broadview

Bean Salad

- 1   14 ounce can cut green beans, drained
- 1   14 ounce can cut yellow wax beans, drained
- 1   10 ounce can lima beans, drained
- 1   14 ounce can kidney beans, drained and rinsed
- 1   14 ounce can garbanzoes (chick peas), drained
- 1   Spanish onion, sliced thin
- 1   medium green pepper, sliced thin

Dressing:

- ½   cup sugar
- ½   teaspoon dry mustard
- ½   teaspoon tarragon
- ½   teaspoon basil
- 1   teaspoon salt
- 2   tablespoons parsley
- ½   cup vinegar
- ½   cup salad oil

Put the drained beans, the onion and green pepper in a large bowl.

Combine all the ingredients of the dressing and pour over the bean mixture. Mix well and refrigerate overnight before serving.

Mary Woodsworth, Saskatoon

Cucumber Salad

- 1   6 ounce package lime jello powder
- 1½ cups hot water
- 4   tablespoons vinegar
- 2   tablespoons grated onion
- 2   cups chopped peeled cucumber
- 2   cups mayonnaise

radish and lettuce

Dissolve jello in the hot water. Add vinegar and partially set. Fold in onion, cucumber and mayonnaise. Garnish with radish and lettuce.

Jean Schropp, Regina

Recipe For A Wonderful Day

These ingredients are not always easy to find, but once you have done so, never leave them behind:

1 cup friendly words
2 heaping cups understanding
2 cups milk of human kindness
4 heaping teaspoons time and patience
pinch of warm personality
a dash of dry humour
the spice of life

Here are the directions for mixing these things; Keep on hand, the results much happiness brings.

Measure words carefully; add understanding to human kindness. Sift together three times before using. Use generous amounts of time and patience and cook slowly. Keep temperature low; do not boil. Add a dash of dry humour, a pinch of warm personality and season to taste with the spice of life. Serve with individual molds. Works best when made by a good mixer!

So here you have it, what more can we say? Follow instructions and you'll have a wonderful day!

Zucchini Salad

3   small zucchini sliced, about 8 inches long
1   small Spanish onion sliced, about 3 inches in diameter
1   green pepper sliced

Dressing:

⅛   cup salad oil
⅛   cup white vinegar
1   tablespoon sugar
1   teaspoon prepared mustard
⅛   teaspoon salt
dash of pepper

Steam zucchini for 5 minutes or until tender, before combining with onion and green pepper. Combine dressing ingredients and pour over vegetables.

Darlene McLeod, Regina

Broccoli Salad

1   bunch broccoli, flowerets and 1 to 3 inches of the stems
12   to 15 fresh mushrooms, sliced
1   to 2 tomatoes, chopped
2   to 4 green onions, chopped
6   to 8 radishes, sliced
2   tablespoons salad oil
2   tablespoons wine vinegar
2   tablespoons soya sauce
1   tablespoon white sugar
½   teaspoon salt

Cut up the broccoli and steam for 2 to 3 minutes. Cool completely.

Toss together all the prepared vegetables. Mix the salad oil, vinegar, soya sauce, sugar and salt in a jar or shaker to make the dressing. Shake until blended. Pour dressing over vegetables just before serving and mix well.

Bob Briand, Regina

Watergate Salad

1	3 ounce package Pistachio instant pudding	1	cup small marshmallows
		1	20 ounce can crushed pineapple
2	2 ounce packages dessert topping	¼	cup chopped nuts

Beat the dessert topping as directed on the package. Add the pudding and beat again. Add pineapple and its juice, nuts and marshmallows. Mix well. Put in bowl and chill for 24 hours.

Debra Dumontel, Regina
Roberta Hodgins, Kyle
Marlene Deshaies, Regina
Shelley Newfeldt, Saskatoon
Virginia Carey, Swift Current
Cathy Biehn, Regina

Layered Salad

1	head of lettuce	1	medium onion, diced
1	cup diced celery	2	cups mayonnaise
1	cup diced peppers	2	tablespoons white sugar
4	hard boiled eggs, diced	4	ounces grated Cheddar cheese
1	10 ounce package frozen peas, uncooked		

Use large bowl or casserole dish. Break lettuce into small pieces. In the bowl, make one layer each of the vegetables and eggs, in the order given.

Mix the mayonnaise and sugar and cover all. Top with the grated cheese.

Chill 8 to 12 hours. Serve. *It's quick and easy.*

Sharon Holliday, Regina

Marinated Salad

1	small head cauliflower	1	14 ounce can pitted black olives, drained
1	bunch broccoli with stems	1	14 ounce can miniature corn cobs, drained
3	stalks celery		
6	medium carrots, cut in small strips	1	8 ounce can waterchestnuts, drained
1	basket cherry tomatoes	1	green pepper
5	green onions	1	8 ounce bottle Italian dressing
1	10 ounce can whole mushrooms, drained		

Wash vegetables and cut into bite-size pieces. Cherry tomatoes should be left whole.

Place all the vegetables in a large bowl, and pour the dressing over top. Marinate overnight, stirring occasionally.

Drain and serve. Serves 8 to 12.

Faye Campbell, Regina

Blushing Shrimp Salad

2	cups tomato juice	1	4 ounce can small shrimp
1	3 ounce package cherry jello	½	cup chopped celery
		1	tablespoon grated onion
½	teaspoon vinegar	½	cup grated carrot

Heat tomato juice, and stir in jello powder. Continue stirring until jello powder is dissolved. Add vinegar. Chill until mixture begins to set.

Drain shrimp and rinse with cold water. Add shrimp, celery, onion and carrots to jello mixture. Refrigerate until firm.

Edith Shier, Saskatoon

Ambrosia

2	10 ounce cans mandarin oranges, drained	1	10 ounce bag of miniature white marshmallows
1	14 ounce can drained crushed pineapple		marachino cherries
1	half pint container sour cream	1	10 ounce can drained fruit cocktail (optional)
1	cup shredded coconut		

Mix all ingredients together. Add cherries and fruit cocktail if desired. Chill. *This can be used as a dessert or as a salad.*

Gayle Thompson, Semans
Beverly Creusot, Regina
Bonnie Wostradowski, Central Butte
Evelyn Hull, Willowbrook
Doris Bell, Regina
Julia Westerman, Fort Qu'Appelle
Darlene Edstrom, Melfort

Molded Coleslaw

1	3 ounce package lemon flavored jello powder	1½	cups finely shredded cabbage
1	cup hot water	½	cup radish slices
½	cup mayonnaise	½	cup diced celery
½	cup cold water	2	to 4 tablespoons diced green pepper
2	tablespoons vinegar		
¼	teaspoon salt	1	tablespoon diced onion

Dissolve jello in hot water. Blend in mayonnaise, cold water, vinegar and salt. Chill until partially set. Beat until fluffy. Add all of the vegetables. Pour into a salad mold. Chill until set.

Yield 6 to 8 servings.

Gwen Veikle, Cut Knife

Fruit Salad

2 eggs
2 tablespoons sugar
¼ cup vinegar
1 14 ounce can pineapple chunks
1 14 ounce can pears, cut up
1 10 ounce can orange slices
2 cups miniature white marshmallows
½ pint whipping cream

Mix eggs, sugar and vinegar in a saucepan and bring to a slow boil. Turn down the heat and stir until thickened. Refrigerate until cool.

Drain all the fruit and mix with the marshmallows. Fold in the egg mixture.

Beat the whipping cream until stiff and then fold into the fruit mixture.

Chill overnight.

Alice Miller, Craik

Ice Salad

1 14 ounce can crushed pineapple
water
1 3 ounce package lemon jello powder
2 cups vanilla ice cream

Drain juice from pineapple. Add enough water to juice to make 1 cup. Heat to boiling and dissolve jello powder. Add ice cream and stir till melted. Add crushed pineapple. Refrigerate. This sets quickly.

Fannie Madrilejos, Regina

Scrumptious Summer Salad

1 10 ounce can tomato soup
1 3 ounce package lemon jello powder
1 cup creamed cottage cheese
1 cup salad dressing
1 cup finely chopped celery
¼ cup grated onion
1 cup finely chopped green pepper
1 cup grated medium Cheddar cheese
1 6 ounce can chicken, shrimp, crab, tuna or salmon, drained
salt to taste

Have all ingredients chopped before making jello mixture.

Heat soup in saucepan. Add jello powder, stir to dissolve. Cool. Blend cottage cheese and salad dressing. Put through a sieve to remove all lumps. Add to cooled soup mixture. Mix. Chill until partially set.

Fold in vegetables, cheese, chicken or fish and salt. Chill until set in 5-cup ring mold rinsed out in cold water.

Serves 6 to 8.

Kathy Keller, Regina

Salad Dressing

2 eggs
1 teaspoon dry mustard
1 teaspoon salt, or celery salt
1 10 ounce can sweetened condensed milk
1 cup vinegar

Combine mustard, eggs and salt and beat until light. Add condensed milk and vinegar and beat all ingredients until smooth.

Makes 1 quart sealer. Store in fridge.

Julia Westerman, Fort Qu'Appelle

Pineapple Cheese Salad

2½ cups crushed pineapple, drained
1   3 ounce package lime jello
¼ teaspoon salt
½ pint whipping cream
½ cup chopped celery
½ cup grated Cheddar cheese
⅔ cup chopped walnuts or pecans

Drain pineapple and reserve juice. Put juice in a saucepan, heat to boiling, add jello, mix and dissolve. Cool.

Whip cream to stiff peaks. In a bowl mix pineapple, cheese, nuts and salt, then add jello mixture and celery. Fold the whipped cream into above mixture. Put in mold. Store in refrigerator. *Make a day ahead.*

Julia Westerman, Fort Qu'Appelle
Rose Carsten, Regina

Cottage Cheese Salad

1   3 ounce package lime jello
1   cup boiling water
½ cup pineapple juice
1   cup whipping cream, whipped or 1 2 ounce package dessert topping, whipped
1½ cups creamed cottage cheese
1   cup crushed pineapple, drained

Dissolve jello in boiling water. Add the pineapple juice. Allow to cool until thickened. Combine the whipped cream, cottage cheese and pineapple and add to the cooled jello (not solidified). Mix well. Chill and serve.

Anita Veikle, Cut Knife

Velvet Salad

1	3 ounce package lemon jello powder	1	4 ounce package cream cheese
2½	cups boiling water	1	cup crushed pineapple, drained
1	10 ounce package white miniature marshmallows	1	3 ounce package red jello powder
½	cup whipping cream, whipped	1	cup cold water
2	tablespoons salad dressing		

Dissolve lemon jello powder in 1 cup of the boiling water. Let cool about ½ hour.

Melt marshmallows in ½ cup of the hot water, over low heat. Add whipped cream, salad dressing, cream cheese and pineapple. Add to lemon jello and let set in a 9 x 14 inch pan.

Dissolve red jello powder in 1 cup of boiling water and 1 cup cold water. Cool until syrupy, about 1½ hours. Pour over yellow jello. Let chill until firm.

Rose Wilson, Regina

Picnic Potato Salad

1½	cups mayonnaise	1½	cups thinly sliced celery
3	tablespoons sweet pickle juice	½	cup chopped green onions
1	tablespoon prepared mustard	¼	cup thinly sliced radishes
2	teaspoons salt	¼	cup chopped gherkins
	pinch of pepper	4	hard boiled eggs chopped
8	cups cubed cooked potatoes		

Combine mayonnaise, pickle juice, mustard, salt and pepper to make the dressing. In a large bowl, put the vegetables, eggs, and gherkins. Pour the dressing over all and toss gently. Season to taste.

Chill at least 3 hours. Serves 10 to 12.

Dyanne Christensen, Swift Current

Jellied Salad

- 1   3 ounce package of strawberry jello
- 2   cups hot water
- ¾   cup cold water
- 1   medium banana, sliced
- 1   3 ounce package lime jello
- 1   2 ounce package dessert topping
- 1   20 ounce can pineapple tidbits, drained reserving the liquid

Dissolve the strawberry jello powder in 1 cup of hot water. Add ¾ cups of cold water. Chill until slightly thickened. Then fold in one medium banana, sliced. Pour into an oiled 6 cup mold or 2 9 x 5 x 3 inch loaf pans. Chill until almost firm.

Meanwhile dissolve the lime jello in one cup of the hot water. Add ¾ cup of the reserved pineapple juice. Chill ½ cup of the lime jello until slightly thickened. Prepare dessert topping according to the package directions. Fold prepared dessert topping into the ½ cup slightly thickened lime jello. Pour over the strawberry jello in the mold. Chill until almost firm.

Chill remaining lime jello until slightly thickened. Fold in drained pineapple tidbits. Pour over jello in mold. Chill until firm. Unmold. *This is nice and colorful for Christmas.*

Ann Bell, Battleford

Layered Cherry — Cheese Mold

1	envelope unflavoured gelatin	1	tablespoon lemon juice
1	cup cold water	1	19 ounce can cherry pie filling
1	tablespoon lemon juice	1	2 ounce package dessert topping
1	3 ounce package cherry or raspberry flavoured gelatin	6	ounces cream cheese, softened
1	cup boiling water		

In a saucepan, soften unflavoured gelatin in one cup cold water. Heat and stir until dissolved. Stir in 1 tablespoon lemon juice. Cool.

Dissolve flavoured gelatin in 1 cup of boiling water. Stir in 1 tablespoon lemon juice and pie filling. Pour about a ¾ inch layer into an oiled 6½ cup jelly mold. Chill until almost firm. Leave remainder of cherry mixture at room temperature.

Prepare dessert topping mix according to package directions. Beat in cream cheese and cooled unflavoured gelatin. Spoon about a ¾ inch layer over almost firm cherry layer. Chill until this layer is almost firm. Leave rest of the white mixture at room temperature.

Continue alternating red and white layers, chilling each until almost firm. Chill total mold until firm.

Serves about 15.

Sheilagh Basky, Saskatoon

Two Tone Christmas Jellied Salad

I invented this recipe to fill a 1 quart mold. It is unique in having the salad dressing layer on the bottom.

1	3 ounce package lemon flavored jello	¾	cup cold water
1	cup boiling water	1	envelope unflavored gelatin
1	cup tomato juice or V8 juice	1	tablespoon lemon juice
		¾	cup mayonnaise
1½	cups total of chopped vegetables, either 2 tablespoons each of chopped onion, green pepper, celery and cabbage or use finely cut coleslaw	½	cup total chopped red and green pepper (substitute tinned pimento if red pepper is not available)

Dissolve jello powder in boiling water. Add tomato juice. Chill. When slightly thickened, fold in 1½ cups chopped vegetables. Pour into greased jello mold. Chill to set.

In a saucepan, sprinkle gelatin over cold water. Allow to soften for 5 minutes. Mix well and stir over low heat until gelatin melts. Cool. Add lemon juice, and mayonnaise. Blend. Chill until slightly thickened. Fold in up to ½ cup chopped red and green pepper. Pour over solidified aspic to fill mold. Chill completed salad for 3 to 4 hours before unmolding to serve. Garnish with parsley sprigs, if desired.

Ruth Griffiths, Prince Albert

Molded Waldorf Salad

1	3 ounce package lime jello powder	¼	cup chopped pecans (or walnuts)
1	cup boiling water	1	cup miniature marshmallows
½	cup cold water		
1½	cups diced apples, skins left on	¼	cup mayonnaise
¼	cup diced celery	¾	cup whipping cream, whipped

Dissolve jello in boiling water, add cold water and chill until slightly thickened. Combine apples, celery, pecans, marshmallows and mayonnaise. When gelatin mixture is of egg white consistency, fold in apple mixture, and whipped cream. Turn into four cup mold and chill until firm.

Serves 8 persons.

Emma Wadsworth, Moose Jaw
Wendy Wuschke, Regina

Sweet Cream Carrot Salad

1	6 ounce package lemon jello (or lime)	1	cup crushed pineapple, well drained and reserving liquid
2	cups boiling water		
cold water		1	cup long-grated carrots
½	cup flaked almonds	1	cup whipping cream

Quick set jello by dissolving jello powder in the boiling water, then adding 2 cups of cold liquid, using the reserved pineapple juice plus enough water to make up to 2 cups. Let stand in refrigerator to partially set.

Blend in almonds, carrots, and drained pineapple. Whip cream until stiff and fold into above mixture. Pour into jelly mold and let set overnight.

Carol Biggin, Regina
Karen Kenway, Nipawin

Tomato and Rice Soup

2	tablespoons chopped onion	1	cup cooked brown rice
2	tablespoons butter	¼	cup cream
3	cups tomato juice		sprinkle of basil
			sugar to taste

Saute onion in butter for 5 minutes. Add tomato juice, rice, cream and seasonings; heat to simmering point. Remove from heat and serve. Serves 2 generously.

Karen Haggman, Regina

Hearty Beef and Vegetable Soup

1	pound stewing beef, cut in 1 inch pieces	½	cup chopped onion (1 medium)
6	cups water	¼	cup pearl barley
1	19 ounce can whole tomatoes	6	peppercorns
		1	bay leaf
2	cups diced potatoes (2 large)	1	tablespoon salt
		1	teaspoon sugar
2	cups diced carrots (6 medium)	½	cup kernel corn
		½	cup peas
1	cup diced celery (2 stalks)		

In a large kettle brown beef. Add all ingredients, cover and bring to a boil. Turn heat low, simmer 1½ to 2 hours or until meat is tender.

Makes about 4 quarts.

Geri Seidler, Moose Jaw

Sopa De Elate
(Mexican Corn Soup)

4	cups kernel corn	1	tablespoon diced canned chillies
1	cup water		
2	tablespoons butter	6	tablespoons crumbled Cheddar cheese
3½	cups milk		
½	teaspoon salt		

Blend corn and water in a blender to make a smooth puree. Melt butter, but do not allow it to get too hot. Add corn puree, cook over medium heat 5 minutes stirring constantly. Add milk and salt. Bring to a boil. Lower heat. Simmer 10 minutes, stirring occasionally.

To serve, place ½ teaspoon of chillie and 1 tablespoon of cheese in each of 6 soup bowls. Pour hot soup over top. *The amount of chillie may be adjusted to taste. If dried chillies are used as a substitute, a generous pinch of chillie per bowl will be enough.*

Joanne Sorenson, Glaslyn

Super Mushroom Soup

1½	pounds fresh mushrooms	2	cups sour cream
1	quart beef stock	2	tablespoons lemon juice
1	cup fresh chopped parsley	5	tablespoons butter
			salt and pepper added to taste

Blenderize all ingredients, heat and serve. You could also add any seasonal fresh vegetables for different flavor, if desired (for example, tomatoes). Also, any spice you like may be added to taste, as well as some red wine to taste. *I picked up this recipe while travelling through New Zealand in early 1978. It comes from a restaurant in Christ Church called the "Hard Rock Cafe". Very nice place — a great place to go for very good food.*

Anita Veikle, Cut Knife

Ukranian Borsch

1	pound spareribs	1	medium onion, chopped
1	tablespoon salt	1	cup cabbage, shredded
few	peppercorns	½	teaspoon sugar
piece of bay leaf		1	cup tomato juice
2	or 3 beets, sliced thinly	1	tablespoon vinegar
1	or 2 carrots, sliced thinly	½	cup cream
2	stalks celery, chopped		

Cut up the spareribs, cover with 1½ to 2 quarts water. Add salt and spices. Cook on low heat until meat is tender and falls off bone. Lift out meat and strain juice.

Pre-boil the shredded cabbage until softened. Add all vegetables to the soup stock and cook until tender. Add sugar, tomato juice and vinegar. Just before serving add cream.

Jill Bihun, Regina

White Borsch

1	small onion, chopped	4	cups soup stock
2	tablespoons butter	2	cups water
2	medium potatoes, diced fine	1	teaspoon salt
		1	tablespoon flour
1	small stalk celery, diced fine	⅓	cup or more of sour cream
1	cup shredded cabbage		

Cook onion in butter until slightly wilted. Add vegetables, soup stock, water and salt. Cover and cook until vegetables are tender.

Blend flour with sour cream. Spoon some soup liquid into it. Stir into soup and bring to a boil. Season to taste with salt and pepper. Garnish with dill or parsley, if desired.

Lynne Hutzul, Ituna

Vegetable Chowder

- 2 cups diced potatoes
- 2 cups cauliflower, cut in small pieces
- 1 cup chopped onion
- 3 cups tomatoes, or 1 20 ounce can of tomatoes with juice, mashed
- 2 teaspoons salt
- ½ teaspoon oregano
- ½ teaspoon pepper
- 1 beef bouillon cube
- 3 tablespoons margarine
- ¼ cup flour
- ½ teaspoon salt
- ¼ teaspoon pepper
- 2 cups milk
- ½ teaspoon dry mustard
- 1 tablespoon Worcestershire sauce
- 1 cup grated Cheddar cheese
- 1 tablespoon parsley

Boil vegetables, 2 teaspoons salt, oregano, pepper and bouillon cube in 3 cups of water, until vegetables are approaching tenderness. Do not over-boil; the vegetables should be firm and a bit crisp.

Melt margarine, add flour, stir in milk and cook till thickened and smooth. Add the rest of the spices between stirs, then add grated cheese and parsley. Add this to vegetables and bring to almost a boil. Serve hot. *This is also a great leftover.*

Bob Briand, Regina

Minestrone Soup

This is a delicious, hearty soup that is easy to make with ingredients you usually have on hand.

- 1 cup chopped celery (the top part with the leaves)
- 3 carrots, sliced in circles
- 3 tomatoes, chopped (or 1 14 ounce can, drained)
- 1 cup shredded cabbage
- 1 onion, finely sliced
- 3 tablespoons butter or margarine
- 7 cups boiling water
- 2 chicken bouillon cubes
- 1 14 ounce can kidney beans
- 1 10 ounce can peas (or 1 cup frozen peas)
- ½ cup elbow macaroni, uncooked
- salt and pepper to taste
- dash of sage
- grated parmesan cheese

Cook fresh vegetables in butter about 10 minutes. Add kidney beans, peas, macaroni, bouillon cubes dissolved in the water, seasonings and stir. Simmer about 30 minutes. Adjust seasoning if necessary. Serve in bowls and sprinkle with grated Parmesan cheese.

Wendy Wuschke, Regina

French Onion Soup

4	cups Spanish onion, sliced wafer thin	1	teaspoon salt
¼	cup butter	⅛	teaspoon white pepper
6	cups hot water	⅛	teaspoon garlic salt
2	beef bouillon cubes	3	slices stale white bread, halved diagonally
¼	cup beef bouillon cordial	½	cup Parmesan cheese

Blanch the onion slices by pouring boiling water over to cover. Let stand five minutes and drain well.

In a large pot melt the butter and add onions and saute, stirring until limp but not browned at all. Add the 6 cups of hot water, beef bouillon cubes, beef bouillon cordial, salt, pepper, and garlic salt and cook. Stir until beef bouillon cubes dissolve, then stir frequently, but gently until onions are limp and tender, about 25 minutes in all.

If bread is not stale enough to be crisp, cut each slice into two triangles and place on a pie plate in hot oven until crisp. Put soup into individual baking dishes and cover with bread triangles. Sprinkle with Parmesan cheese and bake under preheated broiler until bubbling and golden, about 8 to 10 minutes. Serve at once.

Bev Schoenfeld, Regina

Cheese Soup

2	green onions with tops, cut up	¼	cup butter or margarine
2	small carrots, cut up	1½	cups American or Cheddar cheese, cubed
2	stalks celery, cut up	¼	cup flour
1	cup water	⅛	teaspoon pepper
1	chicken bouillon cube	3	cups milk

Put onion, carrots, celery and water into blender, cover and run on high until the vegetables are finely chopped. Empty into saucepan, add bouillon cube and butter. Simmer for 10 minutes.

Meanwhile put ⅓ of cheese in clean, dry blender, cover and run on low until grated. Empty into bowl and repeat process until all cheese is grated. Put 1 cup milk, flour, and pepper in blender, cover and run on high a few seconds. Add with the remaining milk to the vegetables and cook, stirring constantly, until mixture thickens. Lower heat and add cheese. Stir until cheese is melted.

Serves 6 to 8.

Margaret Tysowski, Regina

New England Clam Chowder

6	slices bacon, sauteed and diced	1	teaspoon salt
			dash of pepper
¼	cup chopped onion	1	10 ounce can baby clams
1	cup boiling water	2½	cups scalded milk
2	cups diced potatoes		handful of peas (optional)

Add onions to cooked and drained bacon in a large saucepan and cook onions until tender. Add water, potatoes, salt, and pepper. Cover. Boil for 15 minutes or until potatoes are soft. Add clams with liquid; heat. Add milk and adjust seasoning if needed. If peas are desired, add them to the potatoes as they are cooking and carry on the same.

Liz Weston, Gull Lake

Garden Greats

**VEGETABLES
RICE
PEROGIES
GREENS AND BEANS**

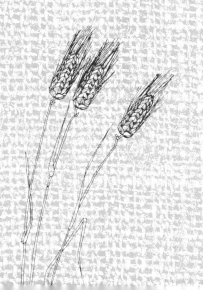
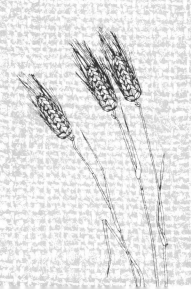

Savory Zucchini

5	6-inch zucchini	¼	teaspoon pepper
⅓	pound sliced bacon	½	teaspoon basil or
3	medium onions peeled and sliced		rosemary
		2	tablespoons catsup
1½	teaspoons salt		

Wash but do not peel zucchini. Cut into slices.

Cut bacon into 1½ inch pieces and fry over medium heat until it begins to sizzle. Add onions and cook 5 minutes, stirring frequently, but do not overcook.

Place layer of zucchini in bottom of a 2 quart casserole dish, sprinkle with a little salt, pepper and basil, dot with catsup. Cover with a layer of onions and bacon and repeat until the casserole is filled, ending with bacon and onion. Dot top with catsup. Bake at 350°F. until zucchini is almost tender, about 30 minutes.

Joyce Hawes, Regina

Zucchini Scallop

4	tablespoons vegetable oil	1	10 ounce can mushrooms, drained
4	cups sliced zucchini		
2	tomatoes, cut in sections	½	teaspoon salt
1	green pepper, diced	¼	teaspoon black pepper
1	cup celery, diced	1	teaspoon sweet basil

Heat oil in electric frying pan at 300°F. Add vegetables and seasonings. Stir. Reduce heat to 250°F. Cover and cook 20 minutes.

Sandra Dowie, Regina

Carrots and Spinach

4	cups carrot slices, cut wafer thin and packed (about 4 large)	¼	cup margarine
		¼	cup flour
		1	teaspoon salt
1	cup onion, sliced	2	cups milk
4	cups fresh chopped spinach (or 2 10 ounce packages, thawed)	2	cups grated cheese
		1	cup dry bread crumbs

Combine carrots and onions and steam until tender. Put half of the spinach in a large 3 quart baking dish or casserole, preferably clear glass. Cover with half of the carrot-onion mixture.

To make the sauce, melt the margarine in a small saucepan, stir in the flour and salt, and cook until bubbly. Slowly add milk, stirring constantly until thickened. Remove from heat and stir in the cheese until melted and well blended.

Pour half of the sauce over the layered vegetables. Repeat the layers of spinach, carrots and onion, and sauce, pressing down the vegetable layers.

Sprinkle with crumbs, and bake at 350°F. for 35 minutes. *This is very good and very pretty to serve!*

Pat Marchand, Regina

Sweet and Sour Red Cabbage

1	medium head red cabbage (about 1½ pounds)	2	tablespoons flour
		½	cup water
salted water		¼	cup vinegar
2	tablespoons white vinegar or lemon juice	1	teaspoon salt
		⅛	teaspoon pepper
4	slices bacon, diced	1	small onion, sliced
¼	cup brown sugar, packed		

Coarsely shred the cabbage.

Measure enough water to cover a large saucepan bottom by ½ inch. Add ½ teaspoon salt for each cup of water, to make the salted water. Add the vinegar or lemon juice and bring to boiling. Add cabbage. Cover and heat to boiling again. Cook for 10 minutes, then drain.

Fry bacon until crisp; remove from skillet and drain. Pour off all but 1 tablespoon bacon drippings. Stir brown sugar and flour into bacon drippings in skillet. Add water, vinegar, salt, pepper and onion. Cook, stirring frequently, about 5 minutes or until it thickens.

Add bacon and sauce mixture to hot cabbage. Stir together gently and heat through. If desired, garnish with additional crisply fried diced bacon.

Note: You may cut the cabbage into wedges instead of shredding, if desired. In this case, cook for 20 minutes in 1 inch of salted water with the vinegar.

Dyanne Christensen, Swift Current

Squash With Pineapple

- 3 acorn squash halved and seeded
- 3 tablespoons dry sherry
- 3 tablespoons brown sugar
- 6 tablespoons butter
- ½ cup crushed pineapple, drained
- ¼ teaspoon nutmeg
- ½ teaspoon salt

Place squash in greased baking dish. Add 1 teaspoon each of sherry, brown sugar, and butter in each half. Cover and bake at 400°F. for 40 minutes or until tender.

Scoop cooked squash from shell leaving a ¼ inch thick wall. Mash squash while warm and add remaining sherry, sugar and butter. Stir in pineapple, beating until well blended. Add seasonings.

Spoon back into shells and bake at 425°F. for 15 minutes. *This can be made a day ahead and reheated.*

Judy McClelland, Regina

Carrot and Mushroom Stir Fry

- 2 tablespoons butter or margarine
- 2 tablespoons oil
- 1 pound carrots (about 7 large) peeled and sliced very thin
- ¾ pound mushrooms, sliced very thin
- 5 medium green onions with tops, sliced thin (½ cup)
- 1 tablespoon lemon juice
- ¼ teaspoon salt
- ¼ teaspoon freshly ground pepper or to taste

In large skillet heat butter and oil until bubbly. Add carrots, mushrooms and onions. Cook and stir until vegetables are tender (about 8 minutes). Stir in lemon juice, salt and pepper.

Holly Hastie, Regina

Broccoli-Onion Deluxe

1	pound fresh broccoli (or 1 10 ounce package frozen)	1	cup milk
		1	3 ounce package cream cheese
3	medium onions quartered	2	ounces shredded Cheddar cheese
4	tablespoons butter		
2	tablespoons flour	1	cup bread crumbs

salt and pepper

Slit fresh broccoli lengthwise, and cut into 1 inch pieces. Cook broccoli and onion in salted water until tender, then drain.

Melt half of the butter in pan, blend in flour and salt and pepper to taste. Add milk; cook and stir until thick and bubbly. Reduce heat, blend in cream cheese till smooth.

Place vegetables in 1½ quart casserole. Pour sauce over and mix lightly. Top with Cheddar cheese. Cover and chill.

Melt remaining butter, toss with crumbs, cover and chill.

Before serving bake vegetables and sauce at 350°F. for 30 minutes, covered. Sprinkle crumbs on top and bake uncovered another 30 minutes.

Serves 6.

Judy McClelland, Regina

Stuffed Tomatoes

6	medium tomatoes	½	cup sour cream
3	tablespoons butter	2	egg yolks, beaten
2	cloves garlic, chopped	½	cup fine bread crumbs
1	cup onions, chopped	1	teaspoon salt
1½	cups fresh mushrooms, chopped	¼	teaspoon dried thyme
			dash pepper

Preheat oven to 375°F. Cut stem ends from tomatoes. Scoop out pulp. Sprinkle the inside of tomatoes with salt and drain shells. Chop tomato pulp finely and save 1 cup.

Melt 2 tablespoons butter and saute garlic and onions 5 minutes. Add mushrooms and cook until just tender, about 5 minutes.

Combine sour cream, egg yolks and 1 cup tomato pulp. Add mixture to mushrooms and onions. Mix well.

Stir in ¼ cup of bread crumbs, salt, thyme and pepper. Cook, stirring until mixture thickens and bubbles.

Place tomato shells in a single layer on the bottom of a shallow baking dish. Spoon mushroom mixture into shells.

Melt remaining butter and mix in remaining bread crumbs. Sprinkle on top of tomatoes. Bake 15 to 25 minutes.

Makes 6 servings.

Faye Campbell, Regina

Sunshine Carrots

7 to 8 medium carrots	¼ teaspoon ginger
1 tablespoon white sugar	¼ cup orange juice
1 teaspoon cornstarch	2 tablespoons butter
salt to taste	

Bias-slice the carrots crosswise about ½ inch thick. Cook, covered in boiling salted water until just tender, about 15 minutes. Drain.

Meanwhile, combine the sugar, cornstarch, salt and ginger in a small saucepan. Add orange juice; cook, stirring constantly until mixture thickens and bubbles. Boil 1 minute. Stir in the butter. Pour over the hot carrots, tossing to coat evenly. Garnish with parsley, if desired.

Makes 6 servings.

Joyce Currall, Regina

Rice-Stuffed Green Peppers

6	large sweet green peppers	1½	cups milk
¼	cup butter	½	cup shredded Cheddar cheese
1	small onion, chopped	3	cups cooked brown rice
1	cup diced celery		sea salt to taste
½	cup sliced mushrooms	3	tablespoons grated Parmesan cheese
3	tablespoons flour		

Cut a thin slice off top of peppers; remove seeds and core. Trim slices and chop good parts to use later. Parboil peppers 5 minutes. Drain.

Preheat oven to 375°F.

Heat the butter in a large heavy saucepan and saute onion until tender. Add reserved chopped pepper, celery and mushrooms and cook 5 minutes longer. Add flour, cook 3 minutes stirring constantly. Slowly add milk and cook until thickened. Stir in Cheddar cheese, brown rice and salt. Mix well.

Use mixture to stuff peppers. Sprinkle tops of stuffed peppers with Parmesan cheese. Bake 35 to 45 minutes or until tender.

Karen Haggman, Regina

Harvard Beets

1	tablespoon cornstarch	¼	cup water
2	to 4 tablespoons sugar	2	tablespoons margarine
½	teaspoon salt	2	cups diced beets, frozen
¼	cup vinegar		

Mix cornstarch, sugar and salt. Add vinegar and water. Boil gently until thick, stirring constantly. Add margarine and beets. Reheat until beets are thawed.

Brenda Martin, Lumsden
Wendy Hudon, Saskatoon

Old Fashioned Boston Baked Beans

1	pound of pea or navy beans	2	teaspoons dry mustard
	water		pepper
¼	cup brown sugar	1	tablespoon salt
¼	cup molasses		speck of cinnamon or cloves
2	tablespoons sweet pickle juice or vinegar	3	medium onions in quarters
		¼	pound bacon or salt pork

Pick over beans, wash and soak overnight in 3 cups of cold water.

Next morning put beans and 2 cups water in large saucepan. Add sugar, molasses, pickle juice and flavorings. Boil for ½ to 1 hour.

Put onion and bacon in bottom of a 2 quart bean pot. Pour hot beans and liquid on top. Add enough water to just cover the beans. Cook at 225°F. for 7 to 8 hours or all day.

Barb Lussier, Saskatoon

Wild Rice Stuffing

⅔	cup wild rice	½	cup sliced mushrooms
¼	cup butter	½	cup cooked diced celery
1	large shredded onion		salt and pepper

Wash the wild rice and soak in water overnight. In the morning, boil the rice in salted water until tender.

Melt butter in a frying pan. Add the onions and fry until straw colored. Add the mushrooms and celery to the onions and cook a few minutes longer. Add the cooked wild rice to the vegetable mixture. Season to taste with salt and pepper. *This can be used as a side dish, or used to stuff poultry or game birds.*

Marlene Deshaies, Regina

Pyrohy

Dough:

2½ cups flour
½ teaspoon salt
1 egg, beaten
1 cup warm water

Fillings:

1. 1 quart potatoes, boiled in salted water and mashed with ½ pound grated cheese. Add salt and pepper to taste.
2. Mashed potatoes, buttered, seasoned and mixed with cottage cheese.
3. Any desired fruit mixed with a bit of sugar.
4. Sauerkraut fried in bacon fat and mixed with pieces of chopped bacon.

Sift together flour and salt in a large bowl. Beat egg and add water, mix together. Make a well in the flour mixture. Add liquid slowly until a dough is formed that is not too sticky.

Knead well on a floured board until smooth. Divide dough into sections and roll out into a large circle. Cut into circles with a large drinking glass. Put a tablespoon of filling in, fold over and pinch the edges tightly, forming a half moon.

Have a large pot of boiling salted water ready and drop pyrohy into it. When cooked, they will float to the top. (About 10 minutes in an uncovered pot.)

When done, drain in a colander. Pour about ¼ cup melted butter over them and toss well to coat with butter. For added flavor, fry a medium chopped onion and some chopped bacon in the butter and toss with the pyrohy.

Serve plain or with sour cream. Pyrohy can also be fried after boiling.

Jill Bihun, Regina
Olga Hill, Regina

Perogies

Dough:

½	cup mashed potatoes	1	teaspoon cream of tartar
2	tablespoons shortening	1	teaspoon salt
2	egg yolks	½	cup lukewarm water
2	cups flour, divided		

Filling:

1½ cups mashed potatoes
½ cup cottage cheese
salt
pepper
½ cup grated cheese, or more if desired

To make the dough, mix the potatoes, shortening and egg yolks. Combine 1¾ cups of the flour, cream of tartar and salt. Mix these two mixtures alternately with the warm water. Let stand 10 minutes. Knead in the remaining ¼ cup of flour. Roll dough out, cut into 2 inch circles or squares.

To make the filling, mix the mashed potatoes with cottage cheese. Add salt, pepper and grated Cheddar cheese to taste. Place one teaspoon of filling on dough. Fold dough over and pinch edges together. Cook in boiling water for 3 to 5 minutes. Drain. Grease with melted butter. *Serve with onions fried in butter, sour cream or mushroom sauce, if desired.*

Makes 5 to 6 dozen.

Adeline Wilson, Archerwill

Lazy Man or Do' Boy Perogies

1	egg	1¼	cup flour
½	cup water	1	teaspoon salt
3	to 4 large potatoes, cooked and diced	¼	to ½ pound butter or margarine
1	large onion, sliced		

Combine egg, water, flour and salt to make dough mixture. Boil 4 cups salted water. Drop teaspoonsful of dough into water, and boil 5 minutes. Makes little balls.

Fry onion in butter or margarine, until soft and golden. Add potatoes to onion in pan. Stir to mix. Add dough balls until butter is absorbed. *These are fast, fun and terrific if you love perogies, but have neither the time or knowledge to make real ones.*

Georgia Hearn, Regina

Rice Italienne

¼	cup chopped onion	1½	cups chicken broth
1	clove garlic, crushed	1½	cups instant rice
2	tablespoons butter	2	tablespoons grated Parmesan cheese
2	small tomatoes, wedged		
½	teaspoon salt		

Saute onion and garlic in the butter for 2 to 3 minutes. Add tomatoes and saute 1 more minute. Add broth and salt. Cover and bring to a boil.

Stir in the rice. Cover and remove from the heat and let stand for 5 minutes. Add cheese and fluff with a fork.

Makes 4 to 5 servings.

Carol Bonli, Melfort

Zucchini Creole

1½	teaspoons butter or margarine	1½	tablespoons flour
3	medium zucchini, sliced with peels	1	10 ounce can whole mushrooms, drained
½	large green pepper, chopped		salt to taste
1	Spanish onion, chopped	½	tablespoon brown sugar
1	19 ounce can tomatoes, with juice	1	bay leaf
		1	whole clove

Saute the onion and green pepper in the butter until golden. Add the zucchini. Mix the flour with the tomato juice and add tomatoes and juice to the vegetables. Add the mushrooms, sugar and seasonings.

Put into a 1½ quart casserole and bake for 1 hour at 325°F. Serves 6.

Brenda Wagman, Regina

Bacon Fried Rice

3	tablespoons bacon drippings	1	cup sliced mushrooms
½	cup green onions and tops, chopped	3	cups cooked rice
		2	tablespoons soya sauce
1	cup diced celery	1	egg beaten
		½	cup crisp bacon pieces

Heat bacon drippings. Add onions and celery. Cook until tender. Add mushrooms, rice and soya sauce. Cook 10 minutes on low heat. Stir in beaten egg. Cook until egg is done. Add bacon and mix.

Nancy McCann, Regina

Lentil Stew

2	medium onions, chopped	2	large carrots, thinly sliced
1	large green pepper, chopped	¼	cup chopped pimento (optional)
2	tablespoons vegetable oil	½	to 1 teaspoon oregano
1½	cups dried green lentils	2	teaspoons salt
4	cups water	¼	teaspoon pepper
1	28 ounce can tomatoes, undrained		

Saute onions and pepper in oil in a large saucepan until tender.

Add lentils, water, tomatoes, carrots, pimento and seasonings. Mix well. Bring to a boil, then lower heat; cover and simmer 45 minutes or until lentils and vegetables are tender. *Serve with warm corn bread, if desired.*

Serves 6.

Karen Haggman, Regina

A Recipe For Living

1 cup of good thoughts
1 cup of kind deeds
1 cup of consideration for others
2 cups of sacrifice
3 cups of forgiveness
2 cups of well beaten thoughts

Method:

Mix these thoroughly and add tears of joy, sorrow and sympathy for others. Flavour with little gifts of love and kindly service. Fold in 4 cups each of prayer and faith to lighten the other ingredients and raise the texture to great heights of Christian living. After pouring all this into your daily life, bake well with the warmth of human kindness. Serve with a smile. Makes enough to serve all humanity.

Casserole Concoctions

**MEATS
EGGS
VEGETABLES**

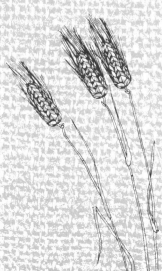

Spanish Noodles

2	slices bacon	¼	cup chili sauce
½	cup chopped onion	1	teaspoon salt
1	pound ground beef		dash of pepper
1	28 ounce can tomatoes, cut up	1½	cups uncooked medium noodles
½	cup chopped green pepper		

Method: Stovetop

In large skillet, cook bacon until crisp. Drain, reserving drippings. Crumble bacon; set aside.

To reserved bacon drippings in skillet, add onion and cook until tender then add ground beef and brown well. Stir in tomatoes, chopped green pepper, chili sauce, salt and pepper. Add uncooked noodles and stir well.

Cook, covered, over low heat for 30 minutes or until noodles are tender, stirring frequently. Stir in bacon just before serving. *Serve with crisp green salad, if desired.*

Method: Microwave

With power select at medium, simmer above ingredients after uncooked noodles are added, for 10 minutes, covered with plastic wrap. Stir 3 or 4 times. *This entire recipe can be done in a 2.5 litre size microwave browning dish with cover (instead of plastic wrap) from beginning to end.*

Makes 4 servings.

Pearl Fahlman, Fillmore
Emma Wadsworth, Moose Jaw

Manicotti

8	manicotti noodles		garlic, crushed
1	pound ground beef		dash of pepper
2	6 ounce cans tomato paste	2	cups water
½	cup onion, chopped	2	beaten eggs
⅓	cup snipped parsley	3	cups dry cottage cheese
1	tablespoon dried basil, crushed	¾	cup grated Parmesan cheese
1½	teaspoons salt	¼	teaspoon salt
			dash of pepper

Cook manicotti noodles until just tender. Drain and rinse in cold water.

In a 3 quart saucepan brown meat lightly. Drain off excess fat. Stir in tomato paste, onion, half of the parsley, basil, 1½ teaspoons salt, garlic, pepper and water. Simmer uncovered for 15 minutes.

In a bowl combine eggs, cottage cheese, ½ cup Parmesan cheese, remaining parsley, ¼ teaspoon salt and a dash of pepper. Stuff cooked shells with cheese mixture using a small spoon. (This is a little messy!)

Pour ½ of the tomato-meat sauce into a 12 x 7½ x 2 inch baking dish. Arrange stuffed manicotti in dish, top with remaining sauce. Sprinkle with ¼ cup Parmesan. Bake, uncovered, at 350°F. for 40 to 45 minutes. Let stand 10 minutes before serving. *Another delicious Italian recipe!*

Deb Fernuk, Saskatoon

Ground Beef Casserole

1	pound ground beef	¼	cup soya sauce
2	cups celery, chopped	3	cups hot water
1	cup onions, diced	1	10 ounce can mushroom soup or 1 10 ounce can mushrooms, drained
1	cup rice, uncooked		
1	teaspoon salt		

Brown ground beef, add celery and onions. Drain off excess grease. Add remaining ingredients and bake at 300°F. for 1 hour. *Oventime can be shortened if rice is precooked while browning the ground beef.*

Loretta Ball, Regina

Breakfast Casserole

2	to 3 slices white bread, cubed	6	eggs
1	cup grated Cheddar cheese, divided	1	teaspoon dry mustard
1	pound cooked bulk sausage	1	teaspoon salt
		2	cups milk

In a 9 x 11 inch greased pan place a layer of bread cubes. Cover with ½ cup of grated cheddar cheese and over that put the bulk sausage. Cover with ½ cup grated cheddar cheese.

Beat together the eggs, dry mustard and salt, then add 2 cups milk. Pour liquid over the other ingredients and refrigerate overnight.

Bake at 350°F. for 45 minutes. *Serve with rolls or toast.*

Makes 6 servings.

Sharon Holliday, Regina

Foamy Omelet

2 eggs
¼ teaspoon salt
⅛ teaspoon pepper
2 tablespoons milk

½ tablespoon butter
ham bits
Cheddar cheese, shredded

Separate yolks from whites. Beat egg whites until very stiff.

Beat yolks until light and creamy; add salt, pepper and milk to yolks. Cut and fold yolk mixture into egg whites.

Heat a non-stick frying pan and spread butter over bottom and sides of pan. Pour mixture into pan and spread evenly. Cook slowly until well puffed up and delicate brown underneath. Place pan under broiler in oven until dry on top. Sprinkle cheddar cheese and ham bits over the top of the omelet then fold over in half and turn onto platter. Serve at once.

Wendy Wuschke, Regina

Souper Skillet Pasta

1 pound ground beef
1 envelope dry onion soup mix
1 teaspoon oregano
1 28 ounce can tomatoes, undrained

2 cups water
2 cups uncooked medium shell macaroni
⅓ cup Parmesan cheese
grated mozzarella cheese

In large fry pan, brown beef; drain. Add onion soup mix, oregano, tomatoes and water. Bring to boil, stir in macaroni. Simmer covered, stirring occasionally, for 20 minutes or until macaroni is tender. Stir in Parmesan cheese and top with mozzarella cheese.

Makes 6 servings.

Joyce Tourney, Regina

Gerrie's Quiche

1	9 inch unbaked pie shell	1	cup milk
4	slices bacon	1	cup shredded Cheddar cheese
1	small onion, chopped		salt
2	stalks celery, chopped		pepper
1	10 ounce can sliced mushrooms, drained		oregano
4	eggs		parsley

Layer the bacon slices, onion, celery and mushrooms in unbaked pie shell.

Beat together eggs and milk. Stir in shredded cheese, salt, pepper and oregano to taste. Pour over ingredients in pie shell, sprinkle with parsley. Bake at 375°F. for 45 minutes. Let stand 10 minutes before serving. *May be frozen for that unexpected company.*

Gerrie Sibbick, Saskatoon

Chicken Chow Bake

2	cups diced cooked chicken	1	cup thinly sliced celery
1	10 ounce can condensed cream of mushroom soup	2	tablespoons chopped green onion
1	8¾ ounce can pineapple tidbits, drained	1	3 ounce can (2½ cups) chow mein noodles
1	teaspoon soya sauce		

Combine chicken, soup, pineapple, soya sauce, celery and onion; mix well. Gently fold in one cup of the noodles. Turn into 1½ quart casserole. Sprinkle with remaining noodles. Bake at 350°F. for 45 minutes. *May be served with additional soya sauce.*

Makes 4 to 6 servings.

Bev Schoenfeld, Regina

Dutch Brunch

1 cup shredded cheese
1 hardboiled egg, chopped
2 teaspoons sweet pickles, or sweet relish
1 teaspoon grated onion
1 teaspoon Worcestershire sauce
2 tablespoons mayonnaise
pinch of salt
6 slices of bread

Preheat oven to 450°F.

Mix the cheese and egg together. Combine pickles, onion, Worcestershire sauce, salt and mayonnaise and stir into the egg mixture.

Spread the mixture on the bread slices. Arrange on a baking sheet and bake for 10 to 12 minutes. *Serve piping hot with an accompanying green salad.*

Juanita Fouhse, Regina

Witches Brew

1 pound hamburger
1 large onion, chopped
1 10 ounce can mushrooms, drained
1 14 ounce can kidney beans
1 28 ounce can deep brown pork and beans
1 20 ounce can spaghetti and cheese sauce
1 20 ounce can tomatoes, undrained
1 cup minute rice or 1 cup cooked long-grain rice
1 teaspoon chili powder
¼ teaspoon garlic powder
1 teaspoon salt
¼ teaspoon pepper

Brown hamburger, onions and mushrooms. Add remaining ingredients and simmer for 15 to 20 minutes.

Anna Clark, Moose Jaw

Chicken or Turkey Pineapple Casserole

1⅓	cup white rice or 1 cup brown rice	4	tablespoons pineapple juice
1	medium size onion, chopped	1	cup mayonnaise or salad dressing
1	tablespoon butter	2	tablespoons lemon juice
4	cups cooked chicken or turkey, cubed	1	teaspoon salt
		¼	teaspoon pepper
1	cup chopped celery	2	cups corn flakes
1	10 ounce can mushroom soup	½	cup slivered almonds
		1	tablespoon butter
1	14 ounce can pineapple tidbits	¼	cup butter

Cook rice in boiling water. Brown onion in 1 tablespoon butter. Mix rice, onion, chicken or turkey and celery in a large bowl. Add mushroom soup, pineapple, pineapple juice, salad dressing, lemon juice, salt and pepper together.

Put in a 2 quart casserole. Crush the corn flakes. Brown almonds in 1 tablespoon of butter. Melt the ¼ cup of butter in the same pan, and add the corn flakes. Stir. Cover casserole with corn flake-almond mixture.

Heat in oven at 325°F. for 1 hour.

Sandra Dowie, Regina

Zucchini Parmigiana

1 19 ounce can tomatoes, chopped	1 tablespoon chopped parsley
2 tablespoons tomato paste	1 teaspoon sweet basil
2 slices white bread, made into crumbs	½ teaspoon salt
	¼ teaspoon pepper
½ ounce Parmesan cheese (approximately 3 tablespoons)	⅛ teaspoon garlic powder
	1 cup sliced raw zucchini
	3½ ounces mozzarella cheese, sliced

To prepare the sauce, heat the tomatoes and tomato paste, simmering gently for 15 minutes.

In a small bowl, combine bread crumbs, Parmesan cheese and seasonings.

Spray a 1½ quart casserole dish with any non-stick vegetable cooking spray. Layer the raw zucchini, bread mixture, tomato sauce and mozzarella slices. Repeat layers once more. Bake at 350°F. about 20 minutes until heated, cheese is melted and zucchini is soft.

Makes 2 servings.

Christina Patoine, Regina

Potatoes Au Gratin Casserole

- 6 large potatoes
- 1 pint container of sour cream
- 1½ cups sharp Cheddar cheese, grated
- 1 bunch of green onions, chopped
- 1½ teaspoons salt
- ¼ teaspoon pepper
- paprika

Boil potatoes in their skins until just cooked. Cool. Peel them then shred into a large bowl. Add the sour cream, half of the cheese, the onion, salt and pepper.

Turn into a greased casserole, top with the remaining cheese and sprinkle with paprika.

Refrigerate overnight.

Bake at 350°F. uncovered for 45 to 60 minutes.

Frances Walker, Regina

Imperial Potato Puff

- 1 cup mashed potatoes
- ¾ cup milk
- 2 tablespoons margarine
- ½ pound cubed velveeta cheese
- 4 egg yolks, beaten
- 2 tablespoons finely chopped green pepper
- 1 tablespoon finely chopped onion
- 1 teaspoon Worcestershire sauce
- 1 teaspoon salt
- dash pepper
- 4 egg whites, stiffly beaten

Cook potatoes and mash. Add the milk, margarine and cheese.

Remove from the heat and gradually add the beaten egg yolks. Stir in the green pepper, onion and seasonings.

Gradually fold in the egg whites.

Pour into a greased 6 cup casserole. Bake at 300°F. for 1¼ hours. Serve immediately.

Darlene McLeod, Regina

Hot German Potato Salad

7	to 9 medium potatoes		dash of pepper
6	slices bacon	¾	cup water
¾	cup chopped onions	⅓	cup vinegar
2	tablespoons flour	2	12 ounce packages bratwurst (or Bavarian Smokies)
2	tablespoons white sugar		
½	teaspoon celery seed		
2	teaspoon salt	2	tablespoons shortening

Boil potatoes in their jackets. Set aside to cool.

In a large skillet, fry bacon until crisp, remove and drain. Cook and stir onion in bacon drippings until golden brown. Blend in flour, sugar, celery seed, salt and pepper. Cook over low heat, stirring until mixture is bubbly. Remove from heat. Stir in water and vinegar. Heat to boiling, stirring constantly. Boil and stir 1 minute.

Crumble bacon. Peel and thinly slice potatoes. Carefully stir bacon and potatoes into hot mixture. Heat through, stirring lightly to coat potato slices.

In skillet, brown bratwurst in shortening, turning with tongs; do not pierce with a fork. *Serve with the potato salad.*

Yields 5 or 6 servings.

Hertha Pfeifer, Regina

Scallopped Sausage and Potatoes

2	cups milk	2	teaspoons instant chicken bouillon mix or 2 cubes, crumbled
2	tablespoons flour		
1	small onion, chopped		
1	cup celery, chopped	¼	teaspoon pepper
1	pound pork sausage meat	6	cups thinly sliced potatoes
2	tablespoons water		

Mix some of the milk with the flour until smooth. Add remaining milk, chopped onion and finely chopped celery.

Brown sausage in large skillet, breaking up with a fork. Add water and chicken bouillon or cubes and pepper. Cook about 5 minutes.

Drain fat, add blended milk mixture. Cook, stirring until thickened. Stir in potatoes and turn into a 3 quart casserole. Cover and bake in 375°F. oven for 1½ hours.

Nancy McCann, Regina

Sausage-Rice Luncheon Dish

1	pound pork sausage	1	package dry chicken noodle soup mix
2	stalks celery		
1	onion, chopped	3	cups hot water
½	cup rice, uncooked	1	tablespoon vinegar

Brown sausage, add celery and onion. Cook until onions are transparent, drain off grease. In a 2 quart casserole put rice, dry soup mix, water and vinegar. Add sausage mixture.

Bake uncovered, at 330°F. for 1 hour, stirring occasionally.

Microwave Method:

Bake, covered at high speed for 15 to 20 minutes, stirring 2 or 3 times.

Makes 4 to 6 servings.

Shirley Gillander, Regina

Cashew Rice and Beans

¾ cup dried kidney beans, cooked	⅔ cup dried parsley
2 cups raw brown rice, cooked (about 5 cups)	3 teaspoons dried basil
	1 teaspoon oregano
olive oil as needed	1 cup cashew nuts
2 cloves garlic, minced	3 large tomatoes, coarsely chopped
1 large onion, chopped	2 teaspoons salt
2 stalks celery, chopped	grated Parmesan cheese

To cook kidney beans, boil in 2 quarts water for 2 minutes, cover; remove from heat and let stand for 1 hour. Return to heat and simmer for 1 more hour until tender.

Saute in olive oil the garlic, onion, celery, seasonings and cashews, until onions are soft and translucent.

Add tomatoes, salt, beans and rice and heat through, stirring often. Sprinkle with grated Parmesan cheese to serve.

Makes 6 servings.

Louise Tunison, Regina

Oriental Beef Casserole

1	pound ground beef	1	tablespoon soya sauce
1	green pepper, slivered	2	tablespoons milk
2	cups thinly sliced celery	½	cup dry bread crumbs
3	green onions with tops, chopped	¼	cup slivered almonds
1	10 ounce can mushroom soup	2	tablespoons melted butter
1	10 ounce can mushrooms, drained		

Brown beef well and put into a 1½ quart casserole. Sprinkle with green pepper, celery and onions.

Combine mushroom soup, mushrooms, soya sauce and milk. Pour over beef mixture.

Combine bread crumbs, almonds and melted butter. Sprinkle over meat mixture.

Bake 45 minutes at 375°F. or until bubbling and brown. Vegetables will still be crisp.

Roberta Hodgins, Kyle

Eggplant Casserole

1	tablespoon olive oil	6	large tomatoes, cut into wedges
1	medium onion, chopped		
1	medium green pepper, chopped	1	medium eggplant, sliced ½ inch thick and peeled
3	stalks celery, chopped		olive oil as needed
½	teaspoon oregano	½	cup toasted sesame seeds
½	teaspoon garlic salt or 1 clove crushed garlic		
½	teaspoon thyme	½	pound grated mozzarella cheese
½	teaspoon rosemary (optional)		

To make the sauce, saute the onions, green pepper and celery in 1 tablespoon of olive oil. Add seasonings. When onions are soft and translucent add the tomatoes. Simmer on low heat for 1 hour.

Saute the eggplant in olive oil on high heat until browned and getting soft. Place it on the bottom of a 2 quart casserole dish. Pour the tomato sauce over top. Sprinkle with the sesame seeds and cheese. Bake at 350°F. for 15 minutes, or for 5 minutes in the microwave oven on medium. *NOTE: The tomato sauce freezes well, so it can be made up in the summer when fresh tomatoes are available from the garden. Alternately, canned tomatoes could be used in the sauce.*

Louise Tunison, Regina

Basic Souffle

4	tablespoons butter	1 cup uncooked and finely chopped meat or vegetable or grated cheese
½	cup flour	
1	teaspoon salt	
dash of pepper		
1¼	cups milk	4 or 5 egg whites
4	or 5 egg yolks	

Melt butter in double boiler. Blend flour and seasonings until smooth, gradually adding milk. Cook, constantly stirring with a wire whisk until smooth and mixture thickens.

In a separate bowl, beat egg yolks and to them add the hot mixture slowly, stirring constantly.

Stir in vegetables, meat or cheese. When cool, fold in stiffly beaten egg whites. Pour into 6 cup greased souffle dish, or into ungreased casserole. Bake 35 to 40 minutes at 375°F.

Donna Flotre, Regina
Marilyn Kolke, Regina
Faithe Prodanuk, Saskatoon

Cowboy Bean Casserole

1	cup diced ham	1	tablespoon brown sugar
2	tablespoons margarine or butter	1	tablespoon mustard with horseradish
1	clove garlic, minced	½	cup catsup
1	19 ounce can baked beans	3	tablespoons vinegar
		salt and pepper to taste	
1	19 ounce can red kidney beans	1	medium onion, sliced
1	14 ounce can lima beans, drained		

Saute ham in butter or margarine. Combine garlic, beans, ham, mustard, sugar, catsup, vinegar and seasonings. Pour into a greased casserole and top with onion slices. Cover and bake at 350°F. for 50 minutes.

Makes 6 servings.

Jacquie Fauth, Regina

Heavenly Hash Casserole

2	pounds hamburger	2	cups cooked macaroni
1	small onion, chopped	1	19 ounce can kernel corn
1	10 ounce can vegetable soup	salt and pepper	
		cracker crumbs	
1	19 ounce can tomatoes, undrained		

Brown hamburger with onions. Mix remaining ingredients and put in a casserole dish. Top with a few cracker crumbs. Bake at 350°F. for 1 hour.

Debbie Mything, Climax

Buffalo Stew

There is a native dish we serve
When feeding many folks
And though you may not go-pher this
Remember it's no hoax!

You take one buffalo that's dead
Skin it, and take the meat
You cut it into bite-sized chunks
This should only take a week!

You add some salt and pepper
Put it in a pot of clay
You bake it, covered, at 450 degrees
For exactly two whole days.

This should serve about two hundred folks
A generous portion of stew.
But if you need a little more
There's no need to start anew!

Just add two rabbits to the pot
It will stretch meals, but please take care...
You'll find some folks complain, if in
Their stew they find a hare!

Olive and Mushroom Casserole

2	pounds fresh mushrooms, sliced lengthwise	1	cup grated old Cheddar cheese
3	tablespoons butter	2	tablespoons flour
1	14 ounce can of pitted olives, sliced	2	tablespoons butter
		½	cup soft bread crumbs
		1	tablespoon melted butter

Saute the mushrooms in butter until juicy. In a medium sized casserole add a layer of mushrooms and sprinkle with olives. Combine the flour and cheese and sprinkle some over the mushrooms and olive layers. Dot with butter. Continue layering in this order. Combine melted butter and bread crumbs. Cover the casserole with the buttered bread crumbs. Bake at 350°F. for 30 minutes.

Val Paulson, Regina

Brown Rice and Cheese Casserole

2	eggs, lightly beaten		sea salt to taste
½	cup heavy cream	¼	cup celery, chopped
⅓	cup water	2	tablespoons grated onion
1½	cups cooked brown rice		
1¼	cups grated Cheddar cheese		

Preheat oven to 350°F.

Beat eggs together with cream and water. Stir into the rice. Add cheese, salt, celery and onion. Mix well. Turn into an oiled casserole dish and bake 45 minutes or until set.

Makes 2 servings.

Karen Haggman, Regina

Marvelous Meats

**POULTRY
PORK
SEAFOOD
BEEF
STEW**

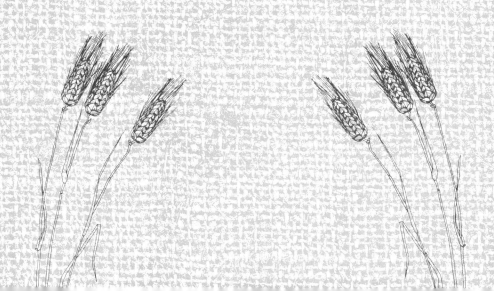

Shrimp Creole

1½ to 2 pounds cooked shrimp, shelled and deveined or 3 7 ounce cans of shrimp	2 tablespoons flour
¼ cup butter or margarine	3 8 ounce cans tomato sauce
½ cup chopped onion	½ teaspoon salt
½ cup chopped green pepper	⅛ teaspoon pepper
½ cup sliced mushrooms (optional)	¼ teaspoon monosodium glutamate
	bay leaf or a pinch of dried basil

If using canned shrimp, rinse in cold water and drain.

In a skillet, cook onion, green pepper and mushrooms in butter for 5 minutes. Stir in flour, cook until bubbly.

Add tomato sauce, salt, monosodium glutamate, pepper and either bay leaf or dried basil. Cook about 10 minutes.

Toss in shrimp and bring to a boil, then simmer 5 minutes until shrimp are heated through. *Serve over rice, if desired.*

Makes 6 servings.

Jean Schropp, Regina

Shrimp Elegante

2 tablespoons minced onion	3 tablespoons chili sauce
2 tablespoons butter	1⅔ cup water
1 pound cleaned shrimp (small frozen shrimp)	1⅓ cup instant rice
¼ pound sliced mushrooms	1 cup sour cream
1 teaspoon salt	1 tablespoon flour
⅛ teaspoon pepper	1 tablespoon chopped chives or parsley

Saute onion in butter until golden brown. Add shrimp and mushrooms; cook, stirring until shrimp are pink.

Combine salt, pepper, chili sauce, and water; add to shrimp mixture. Bring to a boil, then stir in rice. Reduce heat and cover; simmer for 5 minutes.

Blend sour cream and flour together; stir into rice mixture. Heat gently. Sprinkle with chives.

Serves 4.

Georgia Hearn, Regina

Tuna Puff

1	10 ounce can cream of mushroom soup
1	cup shredded Cheddar cheese
1½	cups cooked rice
1	7 ounce can tuna, drained and flaked
1	tablespoon finely chopped green onion tops
¼	teaspoon pepper
3	eggs, separated

Preheat oven to 350°F.

Combine soup and cheese in a large saucepan; heat slowly, stirring constantly, until the cheese melts completely; remove from heat. Stir in rice, tuna, onion and pepper.

Beat egg yolks in a small bowl; slowly stir into tuna mixture; cool.

Beat egg whites until they form firm peaks; fold into tuna mixture until no streaks of white remain. Pour into an 8 x 8 x 2 inch baking dish, spreading top even. Bake for 40 minutes or until puffed and golden and firm in the centre. To serve, cut into squares.

Yields 6 servings.

Karen Haggman, Regina

Seafood Appetizers

2 tablespoons melted butter	1 pound fresh or frozen shrimp
2 tablespoons flour	¾ pound scallops
1 cup milk	1 pound fresh mushrooms, sliced
salt and pepper to taste	
dash of paprika	1 teaspoon buttered bread crumbs (per shell used)
2 tablespoons white wine	
2 egg yolks	grated cheese to garnish
4 tablespoons cream	
4 tablespoons grated medium Cheddar cheese	

Cook butter, flour and milk over medium heat, stirring constantly until thick. Add salt and pepper to taste, a dash of paprika, and white wine. Cool.

Add egg yolks, that have been beaten slightly with the cream, and then add the Cheddar cheese. Bring to a boil.

Add shrimp, scallops and mushrooms. Cool slightly.

When cooled, fill buttered sea shells. Top with a teaspoon buttered bread crumbs and a little grated cheese. (Can be put in refrigerator until 20 minutes before serving). Then, bake at 400°F. for 20 minutes. Slip under broiler to brown crust. *NOTE: This can also be put in a casserole and baked and served with rice as a main course.*

Serves 6 to 8.

Jacquie Fauth, Regina

Oven Barbecued Chicken

2	to 4 pound fryer, cut up	2	tablespoons Worcestershire sauce
¾	cup flour		
2	teaspoons salt	2	tablespoons brown sugar
½	cup oil	¼	cup green pepper, chopped
½	cup onion, chopped		
½	cup celery, chopped	1	cup tomato sauce
2	tablespoons butter, melted	1	cup water
		⅛	teaspoon pepper

Coat chicken with flour and salt; brown in oil. Arrange in skillet or casserole.

Saute onion and celery in butter until clear; add Worcestershire sauce, brown sugar, green pepper, tomato sauce, water and pepper. Bring to a boil; pour over chicken. Cover; bake at 350°F. for 1 hour or until tender.

Makes 4 to 6 servings.

Laurine Forrester, Regina

Oyster Stew

¼	cup butter or margarine	1	quart raw oysters or 2 packages quick frozen oysters
1	teaspoon Worcestershire sauce		
	dash paprika	1½	quarts milk
	dash pepper	1½	teaspoons salt

Melt butter in deep pan. Add Worcestershire sauce, paprika and pepper; stir until smooth. Add oysters and oyster liquid; cook over low heat until edges of oysters curl. Add milk and salt; heat thoroughly over low heat; do not boil.

Makes 6 servings.

Geri Seidler, Moose Jaw

Chicken Filled Crepes

Basic Crepes:

1 cup flour	1½ cups milk
3 eggs	3 tablespoons melted butter, cooled
½ teaspoon salt	

Mix together the flour, eggs, salt, milk and butter to make a batter. In a 7 or 8 inch crepe pan, lightly oiled, put about 2 tablespoons of batter. Swirl it around to cover the bottom and pour out excess, to make the desired thickness of crepe. Cook on medium heat about 1 or 2 minutes, or until lightly browned on the bottom. Don't flip the crepe, but slide it out onto the counter when done. A small skillet may also be used if a crepe pan is unavailable, but make sure the batter isn't too thick in the pan, so the crepes will cook all the way through.

Filling:

3 tablespoons butter	½ of 10 ounce can mushrooms, drained
3 tablespoons flour	2 cups diced cooked chicken
½ teaspoon salt	
1½ cups milk	
2 tablespoons butter	2 tablespoons chopped pimento
2 tablespoons chopped onion	salt and pepper

Make a white sauce by melting the 3 tablespoons of butter, adding the flour and salt and stirring until blended. Add milk gradually. Cook over medium heat, stirring constantly until thickened. Remove from heat and cover with saran wrap, until cooled.

Saute the onion and mushrooms in the 2 tablespoons of butter until tender. Add chicken and pimento, and saute 1 minute longer. Add ½ cup of the white sauce and stir until blended. Remove from heat, add salt and pepper to taste. Refrigerate until ready to use.

To fill the crepes, arrange them on the counter, browned side down. Spoon 1 heaping tablespoon of filling down the center of each crepe. Fold opposite sides over filling and arrange in a buttered 9 x 13 inch baking dish. Cover with foil and bake at 350°F. for 20 to 25 minutes, or until heated through.

Topping:

½ cup mayonnaise
grated Parmesan cheese

¼ cup whipping cream, whipped

Combine the remaining white sauce and mayonnaise. Fold in whipped cream. Uncover hot crepes. Spoon topping over and sprinkle with Parmesan cheese. Broil 4 to 6 inches from heat until browned. Watch carefully. *To prepare ahead, make and fill crepes as directed. Cover with foil and refrigerate or freeze. Combine sauce and mayonnaise, but do not add the whipped cream until ready to use. When ready to serve, bake crepes as directed and continue as above.*

Yields 6 servings, 2 crepes each.

Heather Lynch, Regina

Tuna or Salmon Cups

1   6½ ounce can tuna or salmon, drained
1   hardboiled egg, chopped
1   cup shredded Cheddar cheese (about 4 ounces)

⅓   cup chopped celery
¼   cup salad dressing
1   can of 8 crescent dinner roll dough

Preheat oven to 375°F.

In a mixing bowl, combine tuna or salmon, egg, cheese, celery and salad dressing.

Separate dough into 8 triangles. In a large 8 cup muffin tin, place one triangle in each ungreased cup. Press dough around and up sides to edge of cup. Spoon tuna or salmon mixture into cups. Bake 10 to 15 minutes until crust is golden.

Sharon Luft, Tisdale

Almond Chicken

3	tablespoons cooking oil	1	to 2 cups fresh mushrooms, or canned, drained
1	teaspoon salt		
2	chicken breasts, diced		
2	tablespoons soya sauce	2	oxo chicken cubes
1	cup celery, cut in 2 inch diagonals	1	tablespoon minced onion
		1	cup boiling water
1	to 2 cups fresh broccoli spears	2	tablespoons cornstarch
		2	tablespoons cold water
1	to 2 cups raw carrots, cut into slivers	½	cup whole almonds, toasted
1	to 2 cups fresh cauliflower pieces		

Heat oil and salt in frying pan or wok with cover. When very hot add chicken and saute 3 minutes. Add soya sauce and mix well. Add all the vegetables, onion and oxo cubes dissolved in the boiling water. Cover and cook about 5 minutes.

Blend the cornstarch with cold water and stir into mixture. Cook another 7 minutes or until sauce is thickened and clear. Add almonds. *Serve over rice, if desired.*

Serves 4.

Wendy Wuschke, Regina

Chicken Paprika

3	to 4 pounds cut-up chicken	½	teaspoon pepper
		1	cup hot water
2	small onions, sliced	½	pint sour cream
1	10 ounce can mushrooms, drained	¼	cup flour
		⅓	cup cold water
¼	cup shortening	1	teaspoon lemon juice
1	tablespoon paprika	4	servings cooked noodles
½	teaspoon salt		

Brown chicken, onions, and mushrooms in shortening for 10 minutes. Drain off excess fat.

Mix seasonings and sprinkle over the chicken pieces. Add hot water, cover and let simmer until tender, about 30 minutes. Remove chicken to hot platter and keep hot. To the remaining liquid in the skillet, add sour cream and heat.

Blend flour with cold water and stir into hot liquid. Use as much as required to make a medium gravy of desired thickness. When thickened, stir in lemon juice, and pour over chicken.

Arrange hot noodles around the sides of the serving platter.
NOTE: Beef, meatballs, or veal may be substituted for the chicken.

Carol Biggin, Regina

Sesame Chicken

3	pound chicken, cut into pieces	$\frac{1}{8}$	teaspoon ground ginger
1	tablespoon sesame seed	1	14 ounce can crushed pineapple, undrained
2	tablespoons salad oil	1	cup water
$\frac{1}{4}$	cup sugar	$\frac{1}{3}$	cup soya sauce
2	tablespoons cornstarch	1	clove garlic, crushed

Brown chicken and sesame seed in hot oil in a large frying pan.

Combine sugar, cornstarch, and ginger in saucepan. Stir in pineapple, water, soya sauce and garlic. Cook, stirring constantly until thick and translucent.

Pour over chicken, cover and simmer for 45 minutes.

Serves 4 to 6.

Eileen Woodham, Regina

Super Spaghetti and Meat Balls

Sauce:

½   cup chopped onion
1   clove garlic, minced
3   tablespoons olive oil
1   28 ounce can tomatoes with juice
1   8 ounce can tomato paste
1   5½ ounce can tomato sauce
2   tablespoons minced parsley
1   teaspoon basil
1   teaspoon oregano
2   dashes of thyme
2   teaspoons salt
¼   teaspoon pepper
½   cup water (optional)

Meat Balls:

¾   pound ground beef
¼   pound ground pork
½   cup fine bread crumbs
scant ¼ cup grated Parmesan cheese
1   tablespoon minced parsley

¼   teaspoon garlic salt
1¼ teaspoons salt
¼   teaspoon pepper
2   eggs, beaten
milk to moisten
2   tablespoons olive oil

Parmesan cheese

4   servings cooked spaghetti

To make sauce, cook onion and garlic in olive oil in large, heavy saucepan until onion is yellow. Add tomatoes, tomato sauce, tomato paste and seasonings. Bring to a boil and reduce heat. Simmer one hour. During this hour, if sauce appears too thick, add water.

While sauce is simmering, make the meat balls. Combine the ground beef and pork, bread crumbs, cheese and seasonings. Add the eggs and enough milk to moisten the meat mixture. Make into 1 inch balls and brown in the 2 tablespoons of olive oil. Drop meat balls gently into the sauce and continue simmering sauce and meat balls for another hour.

Cook the spaghetti, drain and put on a large serving plate. Top with sauce and meat balls. Sprinkle with grated Parmesan cheese.

Kathy Keller, Regina

Bierrocks

Dough:

2 cups warm water	1 egg
2 packages dry yeast	¼ cup oil
¼ cup sugar	6 to 6½ cups flour
1½ teaspoons salt	

Filling:

1½ pounds ground beef	1 teaspoon oregano
1 medium onion, chopped	1 teaspoon salt
1 cup tomato sauce	¼ teaspoon pepper

To make the dough, mix the yeast in the water until dissolved. Add the sugar, salt, egg and oil, stirring well with each addition. Add yeast mixture to 3 or 4 cups of flour until dough forms soft ball. Turn onto a floured board and knead in the remaining flour until it is smooth and elastic, about 7 minutes of kneading. Place dough in a greased bowl, cover with a tea towel and set in a warm place until it doubles in size, about 1 hour. Then punch the dough down and chill for several hours.

In a skillet, brown the ground beef and onion. Add the tomato sauce, oregano, salt and pepper. Mix and cool slightly.

Roll out the dough in thin sheets. Cut into 5 inch squares. Place 2 tablespoons filling on each square, pinch edges together. Place pinched side down on greased cookie sheet. Bake at 350°F. for 20 minutes. *NOTE: These can be served hot or cold, and freeze well.*

Gerrie Sibbick, Saskatoon

Chicken Mozzarella

4	whole chicken breasts, skinned and boned	1	tablespooon water
4	ounces mozzarella cheese, sliced	½	cup dried whole wheat bread crumbs
4	ounces thinly sliced ham	½	cup crushed rye crackers
¼	cup flour	2	to 3 tablespoons shake-and-bake for chicken
1	egg, beaten	¼	cup melted butter

Pound chicken pieces between sheets of wax paper until quite thin. Place a slice of cheese and a slice of ham on each breast. Roll breasts to enclose filling or place two breasts together. Dip in flour, then in the egg beaten with the water.

Mix together the bread crumbs, rye crackers and shake-and-bake mix. Roll chicken pieces in this mixture. Arrange in a baking dish and drizzle ¼ cup melted butter over top. Bake at 350°F. for 60 minutes or fry in a skillet until brown.

NOTE: To cook in a microwave oven, arrange chicken breasts on a plate, cover with wax paper, and cook on high power for 4 minutes per breast. Let stand 5 minutes before serving.

Dawna Brown, Hawarden
Judy Hoff, Regina

Tomato Venison Stew

1	pound venison, cut into stewing size pieces	1	10 ounce can water
2	tablespoons flour	6	small onions, cut in pieces
½	teaspoon salt	6	small carrots, cut in half
¼	teaspoon black pepper	3	medium potatoes, quartered
2	tablespoons shortening	¼	teaspoon thyme
1	10 ounce can tomato soup		

Combine flour, salt and pepper, and roll meat in this mixture. Then brown meat in shortening in a large heavy pan. Add the soup and water. Cover and simmer 1½ hours, stirring occasionally.

Add onion, carrots, potatoes and thyme. Cook covered until vegetables are tender, about 1 hour on low heat. If desired, cook uncovered during the last 10 minutes to thicken the sauce.

Dyanne Christensen, Swift Current

Chop Suey

½	pound beef, pork or chicken, cut into small pieces	1	10 ounce can mushrooms, drained, saving liquid
¼	cup oil	1	14 ounce can bean sprouts, drained
1	teaspoon salt		
1	tablespoon soya sauce	1	tablespoon cornstarch
1	clove minced garlic		Chinese noodles, if desired
1	cup onion, chopped	4	servings rice, if desired
1	cup celery, chopped		

Heat oil in fry pan. Add the meat, salt, soya sauce, and garlic; brown quickly and remove from pan.

To the pan add onion, celery, mushrooms, and bean sprouts and fry a few minutes. Add meat.

Mix cornstarch with mushroom liquid and add to pan. Heat until hot and thickened.

Chinese noodles may be added before serving.

Serve with rice. *NOTE: Leftover meats may be used in this recipe.*

Serves 4.

Diana Starosta, Regina

Mini Meat Pies

Pastry:

2 cups all purpose flour	3 tablespoons ketchup
½ teaspoon salt	¼ cup cold water
⅔ cup shortening	

Filling:

1½ pounds lean beef hamburger
1 tablespoon fat or margarine
½ cup finely chopped onion
1 package dry onion soup
⅓ cup pickle relish, preferably green
3 tablespoons ketchup
½ cup leftover gravy, preferably beef, medium thickness
½ teaspoon salt

Mix pastry ingredients together, making a fairly moist dough. Roll onto a well-floured tabletop to make a thin sheet. Cut into rectangles about 2 x 5 inches.

Cook hamburger about 15 to 20 minutes, and drain grease away. Keep meat crumbly and soft. Add fat and onions, and cook on low heat a few minutes more until onions are soft. Add onion soup, relish, ketchup, gravy and salt. Keep filling hot.

When pastry is ready, drain grease or liquid from meat filling, using a colander. Put a teaspoonful of filling on one side of the rectangular pastry shell, fold over the other side, and pinch together the edges to form a mini-pie. Place on ungreased cookie sheet and bake 10 minutes at 350°F. Serve hot. Makes about 5 dozen little pies. *NOTE: These pies freeze well. Just allow them to cool, then layer them between sheets of wax paper in any large freezer container, and take out as many at a time as you want. Pop frozen into the oven, heat and serve in a few minutes.*

Christina Patoine, Regina

Lamb Stew With Dumplings

3 tablespoons fat or cooking oil	8 small carrots, pared and cut into 1 inch pieces
2½ pounds lamb, cut into 2 inch cubes	1 cup diced celery
1 teaspoon salt	½ cup diced onion
⅛ teaspoon pepper	1½ teaspoons celery salt
boiling water	1 recipe dumplings

Dumplings:

1½ cups sifted flour	3 tablespoons shortening
2 teaspoons baking powder	¾ cup milk
¾ teaspoon salt	

Trim off any excess fat from the lamb pieces. Heat the cooking oil in a large, heavy pot. Add lamb; brown on all sides. Add salt. pepper and enough water to just cover meat. Bring to a boil, lower heat, and simmer 1 to 1½ hours, or until lamb is almost tender. Add carrots, celery, onion and celery salt. Simmer 10 minutes longer. Add salt and pepper to taste.

To make dumplings, sift together the flour, baking powder and salt, Cut in the shortening. Stir in milk and mix only until blended. Makes approximately 8 dumplings.

Skim off any visible fat from the top of the stew. Drop dumpling dough on the stew by tablespoons, being sure each spoonful rests on a piece of meat. Cook, uncovered, 10 minutes over low heat. Cover, and cook for 10 minutes more.

Serve in heated bowl with dumplings on top. *NOTE: Instead of above dumpling recipe, 2 cups of Biscuit mix may be prepared according to package directions.*

Serves 6 to 8 people.

Geri Seidler, Moose Jaw

Lemon Baked Fish Fillets

1	pound fresh or frozen fish fillets	⅛	teaspoon pepper
¼	cup water	⅛	teaspoon paprika
¼	cup milk	1	lemon, grated rind and juice
1½	teaspoons salt	2	teaspoons melted butter or margarine
½	cup yellow cornmeal or very fine cracker crumbs		

If fish fillets are frozen, allow to thaw and cut into serving size pieces.

In a small bowl combine water, milk and salt and stir until salt is dissolved.

In another small bowl combine the corn meal or cracker crumbs, pepper, paprika and grated lemon rind. Spread this mixture out on a piece of wax paper.

Dip pieces of fish in water-milk mixture, let drip, then coat with corn meal or cracker crumb mixture. Place in a single layer on well greased shallow pan.

In a cup combine the melted butter and juice squeezed from the lemon. Brush this mixture over the surface of the fish fillets. Bake at 375°F. for 20 minutes.

Serves 3 to 4.

Hertha Pfeifer, Regina

Chililess Chili

6	slices bacon	1	clove garlic, minced
1	pound ground beef	2	tablespoons molasses
1	medium onion, sliced	2	tablespoons brown sugar
1	medium green pepper, chopped	1	teaspoon dry mustard
		$\frac{1}{3}$	cup vinegar
1	19 ounce can tomatoes	1	teaspoon Worcestershire sauce
1	14 ounce can kidney beans		salt, pepper and tabasco sauce to taste
1	14 ounce can pork and beans		

Fry bacon until crisp and crumbly, then drain. Brown ground beef and onion. Combine the bacon, beef and onion in a 1½ quart casserole. Add remaining ingredients and mix. Bake for 2 to 2½ hours at 300°F.

Judy Jones, Regina

Oriental Perch Fillets

1	pound fresh frozen perch fillets, thawed	$\frac{1}{4}$	teaspoon ground ginger
3	tablespoons oil	1	tablespoon light brown sugar
4	teaspoons soya sauce		

In a long shallow baking dish, arrange perch fillets, skin side down, and overlapping.

Mix all the remaining ingredients and pour evenly over the fillets. Allow to stand 1 hour to marinate.

Bake at 350°F. about 10 minutes or until gently tanned. Test with a fork to see if fish will flake and is baked through, but still moist. Do not overbake and do not turn. These fillets may be broiled, if desired.

Serves 3 to 4.

Hertha Pfeifer, Regina

Polynesian Chicken and Peaches

2	3½ pound chickens, fryers	1	28 ounce can cling peaches
1	large onion, quartered and separated into layers	1	tablespoon cornstarch
		1	tablespoon soya sauce
1	green pepper (optional), cut into strips	3	tablespoons vinegar

Brown cut-up chicken pieces, cover and cook until tender. Drain off all fat. Add onion and green pepper and cook until the onion is transparent.

Drain peaches, saving syrup. Into one cup of the syrup, stir in the cornstarch, soya sauce and vinegar. Pour over chicken and cook until sauce is clear and slightly thickened. Add peaches. Heat 5 minutes longer. *Serve with rice, if desired.*

Serves 8 to 10.

Shelley Duncan, Regina

Stuffed Green Peppers

4	large green peppers	2	tablespoons minced onion
1	pound ground beef		
¾	cup bread crumbs	1	10 ounce can condensed cheese soup
½	teaspoon salt		
1	small egg, slightly beaten		

Cut peppers in half lengthwise, and remove tops and seeds. Steam pepper shells about 5 minutes by placing on a rack above boiling water.

Combine beef, bread crumbs, salt, egg, onion and ½ of the tin of cheese soup. Mix well. Fill the pepper shells with stuffing and place on sides in a shallow baking pan. Bake 30 minutes at 375°F.

Remove from the oven and pour remaining soup over the peppers. Return to the oven and continue baking 15 minutes more.

Serves 4.

Pat Marchand, Regina

Hawaiian Hamburgers

- ⅔ cup milk
- 1½ pounds ground beef
- ½ cup chopped onions
- ⅔ cup bread crumbs
- 1 teaspoon salt
- 1 egg

Sauce:

- 2 tablespoons vinegar
- 2 tablespoons soya sauce
- 2 tablespoons cornstarch
- ¼ cup brown sugar
- 1 14 ounce can crushed pineapple
- ¼ cup chopped green peppers (optional)

Mix together the milk, beef, onions, bread crumbs, salt and egg. Shape into small balls or patties. Brown in frying pan. Drain off excess grease.

Combine vinegar and soya sauce, then add the cornstarch. Add brown sugar, crushed pineapple with juice and green peppers. Pour this sauce over the meatballs. Simmer for ½ hour. *NOTE: This is good served over steamed rice.*

Linda Tidball, Regina

Duckling A L'Orange

1	5 pound eviscerated duckling, fresh or frozen	¾	cup, total, of orange juice and white wine, mixed to taste
1	orange, quartered or 3 cups of stuffing	¼	cup cognac (optional)
½	cup white sugar	1	tablespoon cornstarch
2	tablespoons wine vinegar	2	tablespoons orange flavored liqueur or water
1	orange		

If duckling is frozen, defrost completely. Rinse and dry inside and out. Refrigerate giblets to cook later. Stuff the duckling with 1 quartered orange or your favourite stuffing. Lace or sew cavity closed and truss the bird. Roast on a rack in a shallow roast pan at 350°F. for 2 to 2½ hours or until thigh meat is soft. Pour off the drippings and fat as they collect in pan during roasting.

Meanwhile, heat sugar and vinegar together in a small saucepan until sugar dissolves and syrup turns a light golden brown color. Cut 3 to 4 slices from the orange and drop slices individually into the syrup. Turn slices over and lift out onto a sheet of wax paper. Add orange juice and cognac to the remaining syrup and bring to a boil. Simmer 2 to 3 minutes and set aside.

Shred the peel of the remaining piece of orange into thin slivers. Cover slivered peel with water. Simmer until peel is tender. Drain and add peel to the orange juice and syrup mixture.

Skim off the fat from the drippings. Add about 5 tablespoons of drippings to the orange-juice mixture. Bring to a boil and stir in the cornstarch, mixed smoothly with orange flavoured liqueur or water. Cook and stir until thickened. Taste for seasoning adding salt, pepper, a few teaspoons lemon juice as seems necessary. Dilute if necessary with orange juice or white wine.

Arrange duck on a warm platter and garnish with syrup-dipped orange slices and water-cress, if desired. Serve hot orange sauce separately.

Serves 4.

Joan Isaak, Regina

Honey and Garlic Ribs

- 6 to 8 pounds back or side ribs
- 1 teaspoon thyme
- 2 teaspoons oregano
- 2 tablespoons garlic powder
- 2 tablespoons salt
- 2 tablespoons freshly ground black pepper

Sauce:

- 1 tablespoon garlic powder
- 1 tablespoon black pepper
- 1 teaspoon dry mustard
- 2 tablespoons Worcestershire sauce
- 2 tablespoons vinegar
- 2 tablespoons soya sauce
- ¼ cup Heinz 57 sauce
- ¼ cup A-1 sauce (or a barbecue sauce)
- 3 tablespoons white wine
- ½ cup Chinese plum sauce
- 1 16 ounce jar liquid honey
- 3 tablespoons molasses

Place ribs in a large pot and cover with water. Add thyme, oregano, garlic powder, salt and pepper. Bring to a boil and simmer 10 minutes. Remove from heat and allow to cool, covered, for one hour in the liquid.

Meanwhile, mix together the sauce ingredients and blend well. Remove ribs from the liquid and place on a broiler-pan rack. Brush both sides of ribs with sauce and bake at 500°F. Use remaining sauce when serving. *Excellent with pork chops, wieners, chicken or ham. Sauce may be made ahead of time and refrigerated.*

Georgia Hearn, Regina

Boeuf Bourguignonne

2	tablespoons bacon fat or pork drippings	1	bay leaf
6	ounces fat bacon or salt pork, cubed	1	thyme sprig
1½	pounds chuck or buttock steak, cubed	1	parsley sprig
2	tablespoons flour		salt and pepper
1¼	cups beef stock	4	ounces canned button onions
⅝	cup red wine (this should be a Burgundy, but any full bodied wine can be used)	4	ounces button mushrooms
		4	carrots, sliced
		2	tablespoons chopped parsley

Melt the bacon fat or pork drippings in a large pan and fry the bacon or pork over a moderate heat for about 10 minutes. Remove from the pan with a slotted spoon and put into a casserole. Fry the steak in the fat remaining in the pan and put into the casserole with the bacon or pork.

Blend the flour with the fat remaining in the pan and cook over a gentle heat until the flour is browned, but not burnt. Gradually stir in the stock and wine and bring to a boil, stirring all the time. Pour over the meat and bacon in the casserole and add herbs, and seasonings. Cover and cook in a warm oven at 325°F. for 1½ hours.

Add the mushrooms, onions, and carrots and continue cooking for another hour. Taste and adjust the seasoning; skim off any fat from the surface and remove the herbs. Sprinkle with parsley and serve. *NOTE: This makes a good buffet party dish when made in a larger quantity and served with boiled rice and a tossed salad.*

Serves 6.

Pat Zbaraschuk, Regina

Always Tender Steak In Foil

2	pounds round steak, at least 1 inch thick	½	teaspoon salt
½	package dehydrated onion soup mix	¼	teaspoon pepper
		2	tablespoons water
½	cup drained, canned mushrooms		

Centre steak on a large piece of aluminum foil.

Sprinkle soup mix, mushrooms, salt, pepper and water onto the steak. Fold foil over the steak, fastening it to make a leak-proof container.

Place on a cookie sheet and bake at 400°F. for 1¼ hours. (Medium-well done).

Serves 4 to 5 people.

Brenda Martin, Lumsden

Barbecued Pork Chops

1	pound pork chops, about 6 medium sized	2	tablespoons Worcestershire sauce
2	tablespoons cooking oil	1	tablespoon A-1 sauce
¼	cup ketchup	½	teaspoon salt
½	cup water		dash tabasco sauce
2	tablespoons vinegar		

Brown meat in skillet with oil. Arrange in casserole. Mix together with ketchup, water, vinegar and seasonings. Pour over meat. Bake covered at 325°F. for 1 hour. *NOTE: Round steak can be substituted for the pork chops.*

Sharon Nohlgren, Regina

Rouladen

2	pounds sirloin or round steak	2	to 3 tablespoons flour
4	slices bacon, diced and browned until crisp	2	to 3 tablespoons butter or margarine
½	pound sliced mushrooms	1	10 ounce can beef broth
1	tablespoon dry mustard	6	ounces red wine (optional)

Cut meat into 4 to 6 thinly sliced portions, rectangular in shape. Remove all fat and gristle. Pound each piece with a mallet or platter edge, until it is quite thin. Sprinkle each rectangle with some of the dry mustard, bacon bits and sliced mushrooms. Roll up and secure rolls with toothpicks or skewers. Roll each in flour to coat.

In a skillet, saute rolls in hot butter until well browned on all sides. Transfer to a casserole. Add remaining flour to pan drippings. Cook for a few seconds. Slowly add beef broth and wine. Simmer until thickened. Pour over rolls in casserole. Heat in the oven about 350°F. for ½ hour or longer if round steak is used. *This is a German dish. Excellent when cooked ahead and reheated in its own gravy.*

Serves 4 to 6.

Wendy Wuschke, Regina

Chicken Cacciatore

3	pounds broiler frying chicken, cut up	1	19 ounce can tomatoes, drained
¼	cup shortening	1	8 ounce can tomato sauce
½	cup flour		
2	cups thinly sliced onion rings	1	10 ounce can mushrooms, drained
½	cup chopped green pepper	1	teaspoon salt
2	cloves garlic, crushed	1	teaspoon oregano

Wash chicken, pat dry. Melt shortening over medium heat. Coat chicken with flour. Cook chicken in hot shortening over medium heat 15 to 20 minutes or until golden brown. Remove chicken, set aside.

Add onion rings, green pepper and garlic, and cook till onion and pepper are tender. Stir in the rest of the vegetables, the tomato sauce and seasonings. Add chicken and simmer 30 to 40 minutes or until thickest pieces are tender.

Makes 4 servings.

Anita Farago, Swift Current

Stir-Fried Beef and Zucchini

⅓	cup water	2	medium size zucchini, 12 to 13 ounces, sliced diagonally
2	tablespoons cornstarch		
2	tablespoons soya sauce		
2	teaspoons sugar	1	pound cubed or ground beef, round or chuck
1	teaspoon salt		
1	tablespoon sesame seeds	1	8 ounce can sliced bamboo shoots, drained
3	tablespoons vegetable oil		
1	large onion, sliced		

Combine water, cornstarch, soya sauce, sugar and salt. Set aside.

Heat sesame seeds in a large skillet, stirring constantly until golden brown. Remove to paper towelling.

Add oil and swirl to coat pan. Add onion and zucchini. Stir-fry until vegetables are tender crisp. Remove with a slotted spoon to a serving platter.

To pan, add beef. Stir-fry over high heat until well browned. Restir cornstarch mixture; add to beef; cook until thickened.

Return vegetables to pan, and add bamboo shoots. Stir-fry until heated. Spoon onto platter and sprinkle with sesame seeds.

Marion Isaacson, Saskatoon

Oven Beef Stew

2	pounds stewing beef, cut into 1 inch cubes	2	medium carrots, thinly sliced
¼	cup flour	1½	cups hot water
¼	teaspoon thyme	4	teaspoons beef bouillon cordial
¼	teaspoon marjoram or basil	1	teaspoon Worcestershire sauce
¼	teaspoon celery seed	½	cup dry white wine or cooking sherry (optional)
⅛	teaspoon sage		butter or margarine
1¼	teaspoons salt		
1½	teaspoons pepper		
4	medium onions, sliced		
6	medium potatoes, thinly sliced		

Mix together flour, thyme, marjoram or basil, celery seed, sage, salt and pepper. Dredge meat pieces in this mixture.

In a large casserole with a tight fitting cover arrange in layers; half of the meat, half of the vegetables. Repeat layers. Add beef bouillon cordial to hot water and add Worcestershire sauce and wine, if used. Pour evenly over casserole contents. Dot the top with butter or margarine. Cover and bake at 325°F. for 2½ hours. *NOTE: No preliminary browning is required, therefore this is a great stew to pop in the oven in the morning before work. Have the oven on automatic and the stew will be ready when you get home!*

Julia Westerman, Fort Qu'Appelle

Baked Stuffed Spareribs

3	pounds spareribs, cut into 2 pieces of equal size	3	tablespoons milk
		½	teaspoon salt
		⅛	teaspoon pepper
1	cup bread crumbs	¼	teaspoon poultry seasoning
1	small onion, minced		
1	egg, well beaten	¼	cup water

Place one piece of the spareribs in a roaster.

Combine the bread crumbs and onion. Beat the egg in the milk, and add to the bread crumb mixture, along with the seasonings. Put this stuffing on top of the spareribs in the roaster.

Add the other piece of spareribs. Add additional salt and pepper if desired. Pour the water over all. Bake at 350°F. for 2½ hours.

Makes 6 servings.

Geri Seidler, Moose Jaw

Glazed Ham

5 to 6 pound cooked, boneless ham	¾ cup crushed pineapple, drained
1½ teaspoons dry mustard	whole cloves and pineapple slices, as needed
1½ cups brown sugar	

Bake ham at 325°F. approximately 1 hour. Remove from oven. Score fat surface in diamonds, cutting not too deeply because they open up. A clove may be stuck into the centre of each diamond, or ¾ teaspoon ground cloves may be added to the glaze. (The ground cloves give more flavour and make carving easier; the whole cloves look attractive).

Blend mustard, brown sugar and pineapple. Glaze ham by spreading mixture evenly over the fat, upper surface of ham. Bake at 400°F. about 15 to 25 minutes to brown and glaze.

To garnish, use whole pineapple slices centred with maraschino cherries, if desired. The pineapple may be heated in its own juice or in the drippings from the ham, before used to garnish.

Serves 10 to 12 people.

Judy Jones, Regina

Swiss Steak

1	to 1½ pounds round, flank or chuck steak, ¾ inches thick	½	cup green pepper chunks
		½	cup sliced carrots
		¼	cup chopped onion
4	tablespoons flour	½	teaspoon oregano
1	teaspoon salt	½	teaspoon basil
2	tablespoons hot fat or cooking oil	½	teaspoon Worcestershire sauce
1	19 ounce can stewed tomatoes	4	tablespoons shredded Cheddar cheese
½	cup chopped celery		

Cut meat into 4 portions. Dip meat into a combination of flour and salt. Set aside remaining flour mixture.

Brown meat in small amount of hot fat, then place meat in a shallow baking dish. Blend remaining flour with drippings in pan. Add vegetables and seasonings and cook, stirring until mixture boils. Pour over meat, cover and bake in moderate oven, 350°F., for 1½ to 2 hours, until meat and vegetables are tender. Sprinkle cheese over meat and return to oven for a few minutes.

Serves 4.

Karen Pearce, Regina

Chicken Fried Rice

1	cup diced, cooked chicken	½	cup coarsely chopped onion
1	tablespoon soya sauce	¼	cup finely chopped green pepper
½	teaspoon salt		
1	cup uncooked long grain rice	¼	cup thinly sliced celery
		2	slightly beaten eggs
⅓	cup salad oil	1	cup finely shredded lettuce
2½	cups chicken broth		

Combine chicken, soya sauce and salt. Let stand for 15 minutes.

In a skillet, cook rice in hot oil on medium heat, until golden brown. Stir frequently.

Reduce heat and add chicken mixture and broth. Cover, and let simmer 20 to 25 minutes, until the rice is tender; leave cover off for the last few minutes.

Stir in onion, green pepper and celery; cook uncovered on medium heat until liquid is absorbed. Push mixture to the sides of the skillet. Cook eggs in center until almost set. Blend in. Mix the lettuce in.

Serve with soya sauce.

Serves 6.

Cathy Abbs, Tisdale

Chinese Pork Tenderloin

½ pound pork tenderloin
soya sauce
flour
2 tablespoons butter
1 chicken bouillon cube
½ cup boiling water

1 green pepper, cut into strips
1 10 ounce can mushrooms, drained
2 servings of cooked rice.

Cut pork tenderloin into strips 2 inches long by ¾ inches wide. Dip meat into soya sauce and roll in flour. Melt butter in skillet; add meat; brown.

Dissolve bouillon cube in boiling water and add to meat. Also add the green peppers and mushrooms. Simmer for ½ hour. You may have to add some more water if it gets dry.

Serve with rice.

Serves 2 people.

Sharon Nohlgren, Regina

Diced Pork and Cashews

5	ounces pork tenderloin or pork roast	¾	cup celery
		¾	cup onions
salt and pepper, to taste		¾	cup sliced carrots, par-boiled
1	teaspoon soya sauce		
1	teaspoon cooking sherry	2	to 3 tablespoons oil
dash of sugar		1	cup raw cashew nuts
¾	cup green pepper		

Gravy:

2	teaspoons cornstarch	2	teaspoons soya sauce
1	teaspoon sugar	¼	cup water

Dice pork into ⅜ to ½ inch cubes. Marinate with the salt and pepper, soya sauce, cooking sherry and a dash of sugar.

While meat is marinating, dice the green peppers, celery, onion, and carrots into pieces the same size as the meat.

Heat 2 to 3 tablespoons oil at medium high heat. Brown cashews, stirring constantly. Remove from pan and set aside.

Add meat with marinade to remaining oil in pan and cook until done. Add green peppers, celery, onions and carrots. Cover then stir 5 minutes at 350°F.

Mix together the cornstarch, sugar, soya sauce and water to make a gravy. Add to the meat-vegetable mixture; bring to a boil and add the cashew nuts. *Serve with rice, if desired.*

Bosco Hui, Regina

Friendship

There is a recipe for friendship
We'd like to share with you;
The ingredients are available,
The directions straight and true.

It takes one cup of thoughtfulness
With one of loyalty,
And add one cup of faith and hope
And one of charity.

You blend these all with gentle love,
And cheerfulness to taste.
A pinch of tenderness creams well
And never goes to waste!

Mixed in a bowl of loyalty
With laughter shared, full measure,
This provision should supply you with
One of life's most priceless treasures.

Pepper Steak

1½ pounds round or sirloin beef steak, about 1 inch thick
¼ cup vegetable oil
1 cup water
1 medium onion, cut into ¼ inch slices
½ teaspoon garlic salt
¼ teaspoon ginger
2 medium green peppers, cut into ¾ inch strips instant rice
1 tablespoon cornstarch
2 to 3 teaspoons sugar, if desired
2 tablespoons soya sauce
2 medium tomatoes

Trim the fat from the meat, and cut it into strips, 2 x 1¼ inches. Heat oil in a large skillet. Add meat, cook, turning frequently until brown, about 5 minutes. Stir in the water, onion, garlic salt and ginger. Heat to boiling, reduce heat. Cover and simmer 12 to 15 minutes for round steak, 5 to 8 minutes for sirloin, or until desired tenderness. Add the green pepper strips during the last 5 minutes of simmering.

While meat simmers, cook the instant rice as directed on package for 4 to 6 servings.

Blend cornstarch, sugar and soya sauce; stir into meat mixture. Cook, stirring constantly, until mixture thickens and boils. Boil and stir one minute. Cut each tomato into eighths and place on meat mixture. Cover, cook over low heat just until tomatoes are heated through, about 3 minutes.

Serve with rice.

Makes 4 or 5 servings.

Aleatha Schoonover, Saskatoon

Stir-Fry Beef and Broccoli

1	pound round steak, cut crosswise in very thin slices	1	clove garlic, crushed
		1	teaspoon ginger
		1	teaspoon cornstarch
½	cup water, divided	3	tablespoons oil
⅓	cup soya sauce	1	bunch broccoli, cut in flowerets to make 4 cups
2	tablespoons packed brown sugar	1	large onion, cut in wedges
3	tablespoons sherry		

Marinate steak in mixture of ¼ cup water, sugar, soya sauce, sherry, garlic, ginger and cornstarch at least 10 minutes. Drain well, reserving marinade.

Heat oil in skillet or wok. Add steak slices, half at a time if necessary to prevent overcrowding, and stir-fry over high heat until browned. Remove from skillet; set aside.

Add broccoli and onion to hot skillet; stir-fry 1 minute. Add remaining ¼ cup water, cover and steam 3 minutes, or until broccoli is tender-crisp. Return meat to skillet with marinade. Stir-fry to heat through. *NOTE: Partially freeze meat to make slicing easier.*

Makes 4 to 6 servings.

Fannie Madrilejos, Regina

Deluxe Meat Loaf

1	egg, beaten	1	onion, minced
¾	cup milk	1	pound ground pork shoulder
1	teaspoon poultry seasoning	1	pound ground beef or veal
1½	teaspoons salt	5	or 6 strips bacon
dash pepper			
2	cups soft bread crumbs		

Combine the egg, milk, seasonings and bread crumbs. Let stand for 5 minutes. Add the onion and meat; mix well.

Line a loaf pan, 8 x 5 x 3 inches, with bacon strips, across the width of the pan. Pack the meat mixture in the pan. Bake at 350°F. for 1½ hours. Remove from oven. Invert meat loaf on baking sheet, raise temperature to 450°F. Return meat loaf to oven for approximately 10 minutes, to crisp bacon. *Garnish with broiled mushrooms, if desired.*

Geri Seidler, Moose Jaw

French Canadian Tourtiere

Pastry for 2 double crusted 9 inch pies.

Filling:

2¼	pounds ground, lean pork	¼	teaspoon cloves (optional)
2	cups raw shredded potatoes, packed	½	teaspoon sage
		½	cup hot water
1	cup chopped onion	½	cup soft bread crumbs
2½	teaspoons salt	1	small egg
1	teaspoon savory	1	tablespoon water

Make the filling by combining meat, vegetables and seasonings. Cook, stirring until meat is grey and hot. Add ½ cup hot water, cover and let simmer for 30 minutes. Cool. Stir in bread crumbs.

Line two 9 inch pie plates with half of the pastry dough, saving the other half for the top crusts. Pour cooled filling into the pastry shells. Cover with the top crusts, sealing the edges and pricking the top. Beat together the egg and water, and glaze the top of the pies. Bake at 400°F. for 40 minutes.

Serves 12 to 16.

Pat Marchand, Regina

Beef Kebabs

2	pounds round steak, cut into 1 inch cubes	16	to 20 mushroom caps
4	tomatoes, cut in wedges	16	to 20 small whole onions
2	green peppers, seeded and cut into squares		

Marinade:

½	cup cooking oil	¼	teaspoon garlic powder
¼	cup vinegar		pinch of oregano
1	teaspoon dry mustard		salt and pepper to taste
½	teaspoon celery seed		

Mix together all marinade ingredients. Marinate the beef cubes for at least 4 hours; overnight or more is better. This tenderizes the meat, so the longer you marinate, the more succulent the kebabs. The meat should be covered with the marinade and refrigerated until ready to use.

To make the kebabs, alternate beef, tomatoes, green peppers, mushroom caps and onions on long skewers. Broil or barbecue about five minutes, or until done, basting occasionally with leftover marinade.

Serves 6.

Joyce Currall, Regina

Grandma's Sweet Ribs

1	pound spareribs	¼	cup vinegar
	flour	1	cup water
	salt and pepper, to taste	1	cup brown sugar
2	tablespoons cooking oil or margarine	2	tablespoons soya sauce
		1	tablespoon cornstarch

Cut ribs into pieces, approximately 2 inches wide. Cut off as much fat as possible. Dip ribs into a mixture of flour, salt and pepper, and brown in a skillet with the oil.

Mix together the vinegar, brown sugar, water, and soya sauce and bring to a boil in a pot on top of the stove.

Place browned ribs in a casserole dish or small roaster and pour the boiled sauce over top. Bake covered for 1½ hours at 350°F. At the very end, thicken sauce with 1 tablespoon cornstarch.

Sharon Nohlgren, Regina

Schnitzel

6	pork loin cutlets	1	teaspoon paprika
¼	cup flour	3	tablespoons shortening
1	teaspoon salt	¾	cup chicken broth
¼	teaspoon pepper	1	tablespoon flour
1	egg, beaten	¼	teaspoon dill
2	tablespoons milk	½	cup sour cream
¾	cup dry breadcrumbs, crushed		

Pound cutlets to ¼ inch thin. Cut slits. Coat with flour, salt, and pepper.

Combine egg and milk. Dip the cutlets into the egg mixture, then into the crumbs, which have been combined with paprika. Brown 3 minutes on each side; remove from skillet.

Pour the broth into skillet, scraping to loosen the drippings. Blend 1 tablespoon flour and ¼ teaspoon dill into sour cream. Stir the sour cream into broth. Cook and stir until thick. Serve with cutlets.

Makes 6.

Cheryl Haw, Saskatoon

Lasagne

2	10 ounce packages of frozen spinach, chopped, thawed and drained	1½	teaspoons sweet basil
		½	teaspoon pepper
		1	teaspoon salt
2	eggs	1	12 ounce can V-8 vegetable juice
1	teaspoon salt		
1	16 ounce package lasagne noodles	2	5½ ounce cans tomato paste
3	pounds lean ground beef	¼	cup flour
1½	large Spanish onions, chopped	½	cup milk
		2	16 ounce containers creamed cottage cheese
1	large green pepper, chopped		
		2	eggs
2	10 ounce cans of mushroom slices, drained	3	8 ounce packages of mozzarella cheese slices
3	teaspoons oregano		Parmesan cheese

Mix spinach, eggs and salt together.

Cook noodles in a large saucepan until tender, drain and keep separated from one another.

To make the meat sauce, cook the ground beef in a large skillet. Add onions and green pepper and cook until soft. Drain off excess grease, then add mushrooms, seasonings, juice and tomato paste. Mix together the flour and milk and add to meat sauce, thickening the sauce mixture to taste.

Mix together the cottage cheese and eggs in a small bowl.

Grease 2 baking pans, one 9 x 13 inches, one 8½ x 8½ inches. Spread ½ of the spinach mixture over the bottom of each pan. Layer the lasagne in each pan as follows: noodles, meat sauce, cottage cheese mixture, mozzarella slices. Repeat these layers once, then top with a small amount of meat sauce.

Sprinkle generously with grated Parmesan cheese. Bake 30 minutes at 375°F., or until bubbly.

This makes about 21 servings; approximately 3 inches square each serving. *The lasagne also freezes very well.*

Christina Patoine, Regina

Mexicali Lasagna

This is a hot, spicy dish, that makes an interesting variation in lasagna, recommended especially for spicy food lovers!

1	pound ground beef	½	teaspoon oregano
1	medium onion, chopped	½	teaspoon seasoned salt
1	5½ ounce can tomato paste	½	teaspoon cayenne pepper, or to taste
2	tomatoes cut into pieces		dash of tabasco sauce
1	cup water	1	12 ounce package mozzarella cheese, sliced
1	clove garlic minced and crushed	1	green pepper cut into strips
2	teaspoons chili powder, or to taste	½	of an 8½ ounce package of taco chips
½	teaspoon pepper		

To make the meat sauce, brown the hamburger and onion in a large skillet or dutch oven, then drain the grease. Add tomato sauce, tomatoes, water and all the seasonings. Bring to a boil then reduce to low heat for ½ hour, stirring, and adding water once in awhile if necessary.

In a 9 x 13 inch baking pan, layer the lasagna as follows: taco chips, tomato-meat sauce, green pepper strips, cheese slices. Repeat the layers once. Bake 45 minutes at 325°F. Serve with sour cream or guacamole.

Guacamole:

1	ripe avocado		dash garlic salt
½	ripe tomato	2	teaspoons lemon juice
2	tablespoons sour cream	½	teaspoon chili powder
½	green onion, chopped		

Mash the avocado and tomato, then blend other ingredients in. Mix well.

Nona Burrows, Central Butte

Cabbage Rolls (Holushkia)

2	pounds lean pork hamburger		salt and pepper to taste
1	pound lean beef hamburger	1	10 ounce can condensed tomato soup
¾	cup raw rice	3	tablespoons water
1	cup boiling water	1	pound of bacon
1	large onion, chopped	1	medium head of sour cabbage

Cook the rice in the boiling water until tender. Drain. Mix together the meat, rice, onion, salt and pepper.

Separate the leaves from the cabbage head. Cut each leaf in half, cutting the hard core out. Spread a spoonful of filling on each cabbage leaf and roll up. Place neatly in a roasting pan.

Mix the tomato soup with the 3 tablespoons of water, and pour over the top of the cabbage rolls. Arrange the pieces of bacon on top. Bake at 350°F. for 2 hours. *NOTE: If no sour cabbage is available, take any head of cabbage and scald in water with 2 tablespoons vinegar until the leaves are soft, about 20 minutes, and can be taken off the head without cracking them. NOTE: If hamburger is not very lean, it should be pre-cooked about 10 minutes to remove excess fat.*

Makes 5 to 6 dozen small cabbage rolls.

Elaine Kurtz, Regina

Sweet and Sour Pork Chops

6	medium pork chops	1	tablespoon soya sauce
2	teaspoons soya sauce	1	14 ounce can crushed pineapple, drained, reserving liquid
1	tablespoon salad oil		
2	tablespoons cornstarch		
½	cup brown sugar	½	cup minced onion
½	cup vinegar		

Combine oil and soya sauce and rub over meat. Broil until browned on each side.

Drain fat off meat and arrange in a baking dish. To make sauce, combine the cornstarch and sugar. Add vinegar, soya sauce and juice from the pineapple. Cook over medium heat stirring constantly until mixture clears and thickens. Add pineapple and onions. Pour over meat and bake, covered, at 350°F. for 30 minutes.

Louise Sonsteby, Shaunavon

Rolled Stuffed Flank Steak

- 2 tablespoons butter or margarine
- 1 medium onion, chopped
- 3 cups soft bread crumbs
- ½ teaspoon poultry seasoning
- ½ teaspoon salt
- dash of pepper
- 3 tablespoons hot water
- 1 egg, well beaten
- 1 flank steak, approximately 2 pounds
- 2 tablespoons fat or salad oil
- ½ cup boiling water

Melt butter in a large skillet. Add onion, cook until golden brown. Add bread crumbs, poultry seasoning, salt, pepper, hot water, and egg. Mix well. Spread on steak. Roll up like a jelly roll, tie securely.

Heat fat in skillet. Brown meat on all sides. Sprinkle with additional salt and pepper, add water. Cover, and bake at 325°F. for 1½ hours or until meat is tender. *NOTE: Round steak may be used in place of flank steak.*

Makes 6 to 8 servings.

Geri Seidler, Moose Jaw

Buckwheat Cabbage Rolls

1½ cups coarse whole buckwheat
3½ cups boiling water
1 tablespoon salt
dash of pepper
½ pound pork fat or bacon
½ pound hamburger meat (optional)

1 medium size cabbage, scalded
1 large Spanish onion, with ¼ cup of it chopped
2 tablespoons butter

Wash buckwheat and boil in 3½ cups water approximately 15 to 20 minutes until grain is soft and mixture is thickened.

Chop up pork fat or bacon and fry. When nearly done, add ¼ cup chopped onion, hamburger meat, salt and pepper. Mix and fry for 10 minutes. Combine and stir into cooked buckwheat.

Scald cabbage leaves and cool.

Spread a spoonful of buckwheat on each cabbage leaf and roll up. Place in buttered casserole. Slice onions in rings and fry in butter until softened. Spread over cabbage rolls.

Bake cabbage rolls at 350°F. for 2 hours, reducing heat to 300°F. for the second hour.

Makes 2½ to 3 dozen small cabbage rolls.

Rose Carsten, Regina

Barbecued Spareribs

3 pounds pork spareribs (back) salt and pepper

Sauce:

- ⅓ cup finely chopped onions
- ⅓ cup finely chopped green peppers
- ½ cup chili sauce
- ½ cup canned, crushed pineapple, undrained
- 1 7½ ounce can tomato sauce
- ¼ cup lemon juice
- ¼ cup brown sugar
- ½ teaspoon dry mustard

Cut ribs into pieces approximately 2 to 3 inches wide. Arrange in a shallow roasting pan. Sprinkle with salt and pepper. Roast uncovered in a preheated oven at 350°F. for 1¼ hours.

Meanwhile, mix the sauce ingredients together, and let stand to blend flavors.

After ribs have baked for 1¼ hours, pour off any accumulated fat. Pour the sauce over the ribs, and bake, covered, for an additional 45 minutes. Baste frequently.

Serves 4 to 6.

Astrid Hoogendoorn, Regina

Meatball Stroganoff

1	pound ground beef	¼	to ½ cup fresh sliced mushrooms
½	cup milk		
½	cup bread crumbs	½	teaspoon paprika
¼	teaspoon pepper	2	tablespoons flour
1	teaspoon salt	1	cup consomme
1	tablespoon chopped parsley	½	cup sour cream
		1	teaspoon Worcestershire sauce
3	tablespoons butter		
1	medium onion, diced finely		
		salt and pepper to taste	
		4	servings cooked noodles

Combine ground beef, milk, bread crumbs, salt and pepper and parsley. Blend well. Shape into small 1 inch balls. Melt butter in a large frying pan. Brown meatballs well on all sides.

Remove meat; add onion and mushrooms. Saute quickly. Sprinkle flour and paprika over contents of frying pan. Pour consomme in, stirring constantly. Cook until mixture thickens. Blend in sour cream. Add meatballs to pan and add Worcestershire sauce, then the salt and pepper to taste. Heat thoroughly, but gently.

Serve with buttered noodles.

Jacquie Fauth, Regina

Sweet Tooth Successes

**PUDDINGS
PIES
PASTRIES
COOKIES
CAKES
CANDIES
SLICES
FROSTINGS**

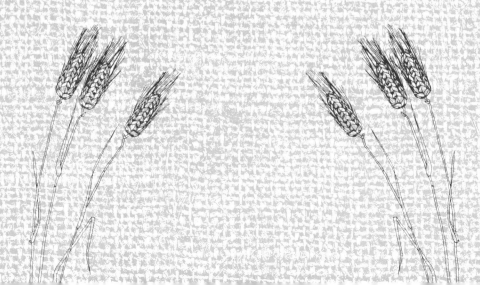

Chocolate Chiffon Cake

¾ cup boiling water
½ cup cocoa
1¾ cups unsifted all-purpose flour
1¾ cups granulated sugar
3   teaspoons baking powder
1   teaspoon salt
½ cup oil
7   eggs, yolks and whites separated
1   teaspoon vanilla
½ teaspoon cream of tartar

In a small bowl, mix together the boiling water and cocoa until smooth. Let cool.

In a large beater bowl, combine the flour, sugar, baking powder and salt. Make a well in centre of dry ingredients and add cooled chocolate mixture, oil, egg yolks and vanilla. Beat until smooth and thick, about two minutes, scraping down sides of bowl with rubber scraper.

In another large bowl, beat egg whites with cream of tartar until very stiff. Carefully fold whites into batter until thoroughly blended. Pour into a large, ungreased angel food pan with removable centre. Bake at 325°F. for 55 minutes. (or until done)

Cool completely on cake rack before removing from pan. Frost with Cafe au Lait Whipped Frosting.

Cafe au Lait Whipped Frosting

½ cup strong (double strength) coffee
2   tablespoons cornstarch
½ cup cold milk
1   cup granulated sugar
1   cup butter (no substitute) at room temperature
1   teaspoon vanilla

In a small pan, stir together the cornstarch and milk until smooth. Stir in hot coffee and cook, stirring until thick. Remove from heat, and cool.

Into beater bowl, measure the sugar, butter and vanilla and beat until snowy white (about 10 minutes), scraping down sides of bowl two or three times. Add cooled coffee mixture and beat on 'high' 10 to 15 minutes, or until all sugar crystals are dissolved. Spread attractively on sides and top of Chocolate Chiffon Cake.

Paula Van Vliet, Regina

Buttertart Squares

Base:

½ cup butter
1 cup all purpose flour

2 tablespoons brown sugar

Filling:

2 eggs, beaten
1½ cups brown sugar
½ cup oatmeal
¼ teaspoon salt

½ teaspoon baking powder
1 teaspoon vanilla
½ cup chopped nuts

Cut butter into flour and the 2 tablespoons brown sugar until crumbly. Press into a 9 x 9 inch buttered pan. Bake at 350°F. for 15 minutes.

Mix filling ingredients well. Pour over partially baked crumb layer. Return to oven for 20 minutes. Cool before cutting into squares. Makes 36 squares.

Cindy Quist, Regina
Juanita Fouhse, Regina

Chemist's Christmas Concoction

The blending of certain substances and compounds in specific proportions results in a product that will please the pallate of children from ages 2 to 102.

1	cup pecan halves	½	cup corn syrup
1	cup blanched almonds	½	teaspoon cream of tartar
8	cups popped popcorn	½	teaspoon soda
1⅓	cups brown sugar	1	teaspoon rum flavoring
1	cup butter		

Heat oven to 300°F. Spread pecans and almonds on cookie sheet and toast lightly (about 20 minutes). Cool. Mix with popcorn in a very large buttered bowl.

Combine sugar, butter, corn syrup and cream of tartar in a small heavy saucepan. Cook until mixture forms a hard ball when dropped into cold water (252°F. on candy thermometer), about 5 minutes.

Remove from heat, stir in soda and then the rum flavoring. Pour over popcorn and nuts. Mix with two buttered forks so popcorn and nuts are coated. Turn out on a large buttered cookie sheet and press into an even layer with the back of a large spoon.

Cool until hard, then break up to serve. *Umm, umm, good!!*

Dennis Sollosy, Saskatoon
Cathy Abbs, Tisdale

Health Fudge

1 cup peanut butter	½ cup sesame seeds
1 cup honey	½ cup coconut
1 cup carob powder	½ cup chopped nuts
½ cup sunflower seeds	½ cup raisins

Melt peanut butter and honey, do not cook but blend well. Add carob powder and mix well. Add sunflower seeds, sesame seeds, coconut, chopped nuts and raisins. Press into pan and refrigerate.

Donna Flotre, Regina
Joan Brash, Regina

Blueberry Slump

1 cup flour	⅓ cup sugar
2 tablespoons sugar	dash salt
2 teaspoons baking powder	1 cup water
¼ teaspoon salt	1 tablespoon lemon juice
1 tablespoon butter	½ cup milk
2½ cups fresh blueberries	

Sift together the flour, sugar, baking powder and salt. Cut in butter until like coarse meal.

Bring berries, sugar, salt and water to a boil. Cover and simmer 5 minutes. Add lemon juice.

Add milk to the flour mixture and stir until moistened. Drop dough in 6 spoonsful into bubbling sauce. Cover tightly and cook over low heat 10 minutes.

Kaye Loustel, Regina

Chocolate Coconut Candies

¾	cup cold mashed potatoes	1	teaspoon almond extract (optional)
1	16 ounce package confectioner's sugar	¼	bar parawax
4	cups flaked medium coconut	8	ounces semi-sweet chocolate

Mix potatoes, sugar, coconut and almond extract. Drop mixture by heaping tablespoonsful onto waxed paper. Roll into balls, and chill ½ to 1 hour or until firm. If mixture is too soft to form balls, chill before shaping.

Melt parawax and chocolate in a double boiler over low heat. The mixture is ready for dipping when chocolate and wax are blended together.

Dip balls in coating, using tongs or forks, and turn to coat evenly. Keep the chocolate coating over hot water while dipping balls. Remove balls from coating and place on waxed paper. Chill until firm. *This candy makes a welcome gift at Christmas time.*

Makes about 5 dozen candies.

Patricia Deck, Tisdale

Chocolate Raisin Clusters

1	8 ounce package semi-sweet chocolate	1	tablespoon vanilla
½	14 ounce can condensed milk	1	cup raisins
1	tablespoon butter	1	cup walnuts
		1	cup coconut

Melt chocolate, and stir in milk, butter and vanilla. Add raisins, walnuts, and coconut. Drop by teaspoonful onto wax paper. Cool.

Beverly Creusot, Regina

Coconut-Date Balls

2	eggs	2	to 3 cups rice krispies
1	cup sugar	1	tablespoon vanilla
⅓	cup butter	½	cup chopped nuts
1	pound dates, chopped		coconut, about 2 cups

Beat eggs lightly and add sugar. Add butter and chopped dates, and cook mixture for 7 minutes, stirring constantly. Remove from heat and mix in rice krispies, vanilla and chopped nuts. Drop by spoonsful onto coconut and roll into little balls. Store covered. *These freeze well.*

Linda Tidball, Regina

Chocolate Cherry Swirl Cake

¾	cup butter	3	cups flour
2	cups sugar	2	teaspoons baking soda
1	pint container sour cream	1	teaspoon baking powder
3	eggs, slightly beaten	¾	teaspoon salt
½	cup marachino cherry juice	3	squares unsweetened chocolate, melted
1½	teaspoons almond extract	1	cup marachino cherries, chopped

Cream butter and sugar together. Add sour cream, eggs, juice and almond extract. Sift together flour, baking soda, baking powder and salt and add to first mixture, mixing well.

Split dough in half and add melted chocolate to one half and cherries to the other half. In a greased and floured bundt pan make a layer of chocolate dough, then cherry dough, and repeat layers. Swirl with a knife.

Bake at 350°F. for 1 hour.

Betty Dobson, Regina

Chocolate Mint Bars

⅔ cup butter
3 squares semi-sweet chocolate
2 cups brown sugar
3 eggs
1 teaspoon vanilla
1¼ cups flour
1 teaspoon baking powder
¼ teaspoon salt

Melt the butter and chocolate together in the top of a double boiler; remove from heat. Add the brown sugar, eggs and vanilla to the butter-chocolate mixture and blend well. Sift the dry ingredients together, add, and blend into the chocolate mixture, mixing well. Spread evenly in a greased 9 x 13 inch pan. Bake at 350°F. for 25 to 30 minutes. Cool thoroughly; then top with Mint Frosting.

Mint Frosting:

½ cup butter, softened
3 tablespoons milk
3 tablespoons vanilla custard powder
2 cups icing sugar
½ teaspoon peppermint extract
Green food coloring

Combine all ingredients, except food coloring, and mix until smooth. Tint the mixture with a few drops of green food coloring until the desired shade of green is obtained. Spread the frosting over the chilled bars. Chill and then add the Chocolate Glaze.

Chocolate Glaze:

3 squares semi-sweet chocolate
3 tablespoons butter

Melt the chocolate and butter together. Drizzle the chocolate over the chilled, firm frosting, spreading it gently with a spatula until the surface is covered.

Chill and cut into squares to serve.

Lois Olson, Regina

Luscious Orange Sponge Cake

Cake:

1	cup flour	¾	cup sugar
1	teaspoon baking powder	½	cup orange juice
¼	teaspoon salt	½	teaspoon orange extract
3	eggs	½	cup ground walnuts

Filling and Frosting:

1   cup sugar
⅓   cup flour
3   egg yolks
¼   grated orange rind
1   tablespoon lemon juice
dash salt

½   cup + 3 tablespoons orange juice
2   cups heavy cream, whipped
1   cup chopped walnuts

Grease a 15 x 10 x 1 inch jelly roll pan. Line with wax paper and grease again. Preheat oven to 375°F.

Combine flour, baking powder and salt.

Beat eggs about 5 minutes. Gradually add sugar and beat 2 minutes more. Blend in orange juice and extract. Fold into dry ingredients. Add the ground walnuts. Spread evenly in prepared pan. Bake for 15 minutes. Turn onto a towel sprinkled with icing sugar to cool.

For filling, combine sugar, flour and egg yolks in top of a double boiler; beat. Stir in orange rind, juices and salt. Place over simmering water. Cook, stirring constantly, until thickened, about twenty minutes. Cool over ice water. Stir.

Cut cake in three equal pieces crosswise. Fold orange mixture into cream. Spread filling between layers, on sides and on top. Cover sides with walnuts.

Joyce Kirsch, Regina

Light Christmas Cake

½ pound butter	3 cups flour
1½ cups white sugar	1 cup milk
5 eggs, separated	1 teaspoon baking powder
½ pound walnuts, chopped	¼ teaspoon salt
½ pound mixed peel	1 teaspoon lemon extract
½ pound candied cherries	
½ pound white sultana raisins	

Cream butter, add sugar slowly, creaming well. Add well beaten egg yolks. Before starting to mix cake, chop walnuts, peel and candied cherries. Wash raisins and sift 1 cup of flour over fruit, peel and nuts.

Add milk to butter, sugar and egg mixture. Sift remaining 2 cups of flour with baking powder and salt; add to mixture. Add fruit to cake batter.

Beat egg whites until stiff but not dry, and fold in with the lemon extract into cake batter. Bake in a moderate oven (350°F.) for 2 hours in an ungreased angel food pan. *I have used this recipe for 30 years and have had many compliments on it. Most people tire of the heavy, dark fruit cakes.*

Mary Klien, Maple Creek

Boiled Raisin Cake

½ cup butter	1½ cups flour
1 cup brown sugar	1 teaspoon cinnamon
2 eggs	1 cup raisins
1 teaspoon baking soda	1 cup boiling water
1 tablespoon water	

Cream butter and sugar. Add eggs and mix well. Dissolve the baking soda in the tablespoon of water, and stir into the sugar mixture. Add flour and cinnamon, and mix thoroughly.

Cook the raisins in the boiling water until they are plump. Add raisins and water to the flour mixture while still hot. Mix well.

Pour into a 9 x 9 inch pan and bake at 350°F. for 25 to 30 minutes, or until done. Let cool. Frost with Caramel Frosting.

Caramel Frosting

1 cup brown sugar	3 tablespoons cream or canned milk
3 tablespoons butter	
½ teaspoon vanilla	

Combine brown sugar, butter and cream in a saucepan and bring to a puffy boil. Remove from the heat and cool. Beat and add vanilla. Frost cake.

Shelley Duncan, Saskatoon

Cottage Cheese Cake

2 cups dried bread or cracker crumbs	3 cups dry curd cottage cheese
⅔ cup brown sugar	4 eggs
½ cup butter	3 tablespoons flour
2 teaspoons cinnamon	½ teaspoon vanilla
1 cup sugar	

Mix together the crumbs, brown sugar, butter and cinnamon.

Mix together the cottage cheese, sugar, eggs, flour and vanilla.

Spread half the crumb mixture in an 8 x 8 inch pan, and cover with the pudding mixture. Cover with the remaining crumbs.

Bake at 350°F. for 25 minutes.

Brenda Wagman, Regina

Icelandic Christmas Cake

Filling:

1	pound prunes	1	tablespoon cinnamon
¾	cup sugar	1	tablespoon vanilla
½	cup prune juice		

1	cup butter or margarine	4	cups flour
1½	cups white sugar	3	tablespoons cream
2	eggs	1½	teaspoons almond extract
1	teaspoon baking powder		

Cook prunes until tender. Pit and mash. Add sugar, juice, cinnamon and vanilla. Mix well.

Cream butter and sugar; add beaten eggs. Sift together baking powder and flour and add to butter mixture. Add cream and almond extract and work into a soft dough. Divide dough into seven equal parts. Pat dough into each of seven 8 inch pie pan bottoms and bake at 375°F. until a light brown color is noted. Do not overbake. Cool crusts slightly and lift out of pans.

When all portions are cooled, layer with prune filling ending with a crust on top. Wrap in plastic and foil and age for a couple of weeks. This will moisten the cake. *Although this cake is named a Christmas cake, it will be enjoyed any time of the year.*

Liz Weston, Gull Lake
Ann Bell, Battleford

Banana Flambe

¼ cup butter		Bananas (¼ per person)
½ cup brown sugar		½ cup white rum
½ teaspoon cinnamon		

Mix butter, sugar and cinnamon in pan and stir over low heat until a smooth syrup results.

Quarter bananas. Baste with syrup 3 to 4 minutes. Heat ½ cup rum in separate pan until warm. Pour over bananas and light. Baste until flame dies. Serve with rum ice cream, if desired. *NOTE: Your favorite liquor may be substituted for the rum. This is a simple recipe that seems fancy. Especially effective if you flame the bananas at the table.*

Nancy McCann, Regina

Banana Crunch Cake

½	cup vegetable shortening	1	cup ground oat flour (or prepare a substitute by blending 1¼ cups rolled oats for 1 cup of oat flour)
⅔	cup sugar		
1	cup mashed banana		
2	eggs		
1	teaspoon vanilla		
¾	cup all-purpose flour	1	teaspoon baking soda
1	teaspoon salt	½	cup chopped nuts

Oat Crunch:

¾	cup rolled oats	2	tablespoons butter, melted
⅓	cup firmly packed brown sugar	2	tablespoons chopped nuts

For the cake, beat together shortening and sugar until light and fluffy. Blend in banana, eggs and vanilla. Gradually add combined dry ingredients, mixing well after each addition. Stir in nuts. Pour into a greased 8 inch square baking pan.

For oat crunch, combine all ingredients and mix well. Sprinkle evenly over batter. Bake in preheated moderate oven (350°F.) for 35 to 40 minutes.

Georgia Hearn, Regina

Streusel Crumb Cake

3 eggs
1½ cups packed brown sugar
1 teaspoon vanilla
1¾ cups flour
2 teaspoons baking powder
½ teaspoon salt
¾ cup milk
3 tablespoons butter or margarine, melted

Streusel Filling:

1 cup of any crunchy-nut cereal
2 tablespoons butter or margarine, melted
½ cup packed brown sugar
½ teaspoon cinnamon

Frosting:

1 cup icing sugar
5 teaspoons milk
¼ teaspoon vanilla

Beat eggs together until thick and lemon-colored. Gradually add sugar, beating until light and fluffy. Blend in vanilla. Sift together flour, baking powder and salt. Add to egg mixture; blend well. Scald milk. Add hot milk and melted butter or margarine to egg mixture. Pour into a greased 9 x 13 inch pan.

To make filling, combine all ingredients until cereal is well coated. Sprinkle mixture over cake batter. Bake in a preheated moderate oven (350°F.) for 30 to 35 minutes.

Mix frosting ingredients together and drizzle over cooled cake.

Cindy Quist, Regina

Grasshopper Cake

2	egg whites	⅓	cup salad oil
½	cup white sugar	1	cup buttermilk
1¾	cups all-purpose flour	2	egg yolks
1	cup white sugar	2	squares unsweetened chocolate, melted
¾	teaspoon baking soda		
1	teaspoon salt		

Beat egg whites until foamy. Add ½ cup sugar, 1 tablespoon at a time, beating well until stiff and glossy.

Sift flour, 1 cup sugar, baking soda and salt together. Add oil and half of the buttermilk. Beat 1 minute at medium speed; then add remaining buttermilk, egg yolks and the chocolate. Beat 1 minute. Add egg white mixture and fold together.

Put into 2 greased 8 inch round layer cake pans and bake for 30 minutes at 350°F. Cool on racks. Split each layer into 2 thin layers with a large cutting knife, making sure that all four layers are reasonably level (trim cake if necessary). Add cream between each layer, and on top and sides of assembled cake. Chill several hours, and keep refrigerated while being used.

Grasshopper Cream:

1	envelope unflavored gelatin	½	cup green creme de menthe
¼	cup cold water	⅓	cup white creme de cacao
1	pint whipping cream		

Mix the gelatin and cold water and let stand for 5 minutes.

Heat the creme de menthe and creme de cacao, but don't boil them. Then add the gelatin and dissolve. Cool, but don't chill.

Whip the whipping cream until stiff peaks form. Fold in the liqueur mixture. Chill 15 minutes, or until spreadable. Add to cake layers as instructed.

Laurine Forrester, Regina

Mabel's Harvey Wallbanger Cake

1	2 layer orange cake mix	½	cup cooking oil
1	3¾ ounce package instant vanilla pudding	4	ounces liqueur Galliano
		1	ounce vodka
4	eggs	4	ounces orange juice

Combine cake mix and pudding in large bowl. Blend in eggs, cooking oil, liqueur Galliano, vodka, and orange juice. Mix ingredients until smooth.

Pour into a greased and floured 10 inch tube pan. Bake 45 minutes at 350°F. Cool 10 minutes, remove from pan and pour on glaze while cake is still warm.

Glaze:

1	cup confectioner's sugar	1	ounce vodka
1	ounce liqueur Galliano	1	ounce orange juice

Combine all ingredients in a bowl and blend. Drizzle over warm cake.

Provincial Lab Staff, Regina

Chocolate Date Cake

1¼	cups boiling water	½	cup cocoa
2	cups chopped dates	2¾	cups flour
½	cup butter	2	teaspoons baking powder
2	cups brown sugar	2	teaspoons baking soda
2	eggs	¼	teaspoon salt
1	teaspoon vanilla	⅓	cup water

Pour boiling water over dates.

Cream butter, add sugar and mix well. Add eggs, vanilla and cocoa. Blend well and add dates and water. Add flour, baking powder, baking soda, salt and water. Pour into 2 greased loaf pans. Bake at 350°F. for 45 to 60 minutes. *This cake keeps in the fridge very well. Slice and eat as it is or with butter. It is very moist.*

Shirley Wiebe, Saskatoon

Cherry Cheesecake

1½	cups fine graham wafer crumbs	½	teaspoon vanilla
¼	cup butter	1	8 ounce package cream cheese
1	tablespoon sugar	½	cup icing sugar
1	package whipped topping	1	19 ounce can cherry pie filling
½	cup cold milk		

Combine graham wafer crumbs, butter and sugar and blend thoroughly using fingers. Press evenly over bottom of a 13 x 9 inch pan.

Prepare whipped topping by beating it with the milk and vanilla until stiff. Mash cream cheese and add to topping, beating well until thoroughly blended. Add icing sugar; mix and spread over crumb crust.

Carefully spoon the cherry pie filling over top. Spread thinly. Chill 4 hours before serving.

Serves 8 to 10.

Beverly Creusot, Regina
Aleatha Schoonover, Saskatoon
Audrey Toews, Regina
Lorna Bennett, Richardson

Shortbread Layer Cake

½ pound butter
½ cup white sugar
1 egg
2½ cups flour
½ teaspoon baking powder
pinch of salt

1 teaspoon vanilla
2 6 ounce packages chocolate pudding
6 cups milk
chocolate icing

Cream butter and sugar together. Add the egg and mix well. Combine flour, baking powder and salt and add to first mixture. Stir in vanilla.

Divide dough evenly into five parts and press into five 8 or 9 inch round pans, that are well greased and floured. Bake at 275°F. until light brown, but not crisp. Allow to cool slightly before removing from pans. Invert pans gently and remove carefully so as not to break up the shortbread.

Add the milk to the chocolate pudding mix and cook according to package directions, allowing it to thicken as much as possible. Chill.

To assemble cake, place bottom layer of shortbread on a plate, and cover with ¼ of the pudding, leaving a space of ½ to 1 inch around the edge. Continue to layer the shortbread and pudding, ending with the last shortbread layer. Ice the cake with your favorite chocolate icing and it's a birthday delight!

When finished, this cake is only 2 to 3 inches high.

Marsha Ackerman, Regina

Bakery Shop Icing

½ cup butter
6 tablespoons shortening
1 cup white sugar

2 teaspoons vanilla
1 tablespoon cornstarch
½ cup warm milk

Cream butter, shortening, sugar and vanilla together in a large bowl. Stir cornstarch into milk and add to sugar mixture. Beat everything at low speed until all ingredients are blended. Beat at medium speed for 5 to 7 minutes until the icing is creamy smooth and of desired consistency. *NOTE: This icing will appear curdled at first but don't give up. As you continue to beat it, it becomes smooth.*

Liz Weston, Gull Lake

Beet and Carrot Cake

Delicious as well as nutritious!

2	cups whole wheat flour	3	cups grated vegetables (half carrots, half beets, or as desired)
¼	cup wheat bran		
¼	cup wheat germ		
2	cups brown sugar	1½	cups chopped walnuts
2	teaspoons cinnamon	1	cup raisins or dates (or half of each)
1	teaspoon salt		
5	lightly beaten eggs	1	cup coconut
1½	cups oil	2	teaspoons baking soda

Mix the flour, wheat bran, wheat germ, brown sugar, cinnamon and salt together with fingers until lumps in sugar are gone.

Add beaten eggs, then oil. Stir in grated vegetables, nuts, raisins or dates and coconut. Finally, add the baking soda.

Butter and wax paper line a 9 x 13 inch pan. Bake at 350°F. for 1 hour, and for 15 minutes more at 300°F. Store covered for a few days.

Deb Fernuk, Saskatoon
Muriel Barsaloux, Saskatoon

Tomato Soup Cake

2	tablespoons butter	1½	cups flour
1	cup white sugar	1	teaspoon cinnamon
1	egg	½	teaspoon cloves
1	teaspoon baking soda	¾	cup chopped nuts
1	10 ounce can tomato soup	1	cup chopped dates or ½ cup raisins

Cream together butter and sugar. Add egg and beat well. Dissolve baking soda in tomato soup. Sift together flour, cinnamon and cloves and add alternately with soup to creamed mixture. Add nuts and dates or raisins and mix well.

Bake in an 8 inch square pan for 1 hour at 350°F.

Cheryl Howe, Regina

Uncooked Marshmallow Frosting

1	egg white	⅓	cup corn syrup
⅛	teaspoon salt	½	teaspoon vanilla
2	tablespoons white sugar		

Beat together the egg white with the salt and sugar until fluffy. Add corn syrup slowly and continue beating until frosting stands in very firm peaks. Fold in vanilla. *Although this frosting contains no marshmallows, it has the consistency of a cooked marshmallow frosting!*

Makes enough to frost a 9 x 13 inch cake.

Jacquie Fauth, Regina

Happiness Cake

To 2 cups of smiles
(Make that a cup of large size)
Add two teaspoons of laughter
And then it will rise.

In one cup of words,
Cheery and gay
You need add a teaspoon of kindness
They say.

Mix these ingredients well to bring out the flavour,
The cake you've prepared is now ready to savor.
Serve in full measure to those you hold dear
And you'll be a success, any time of the year.

Dutch Cookies

Strop Waffles (a syrup filled cookie).

1	cup butter	2	teaspoons cinnamon
1	cup white sugar	1	teaspoon vanilla
1	egg	2	cups flour
½	teaspoon salt		

Cream butter and sugar. Add egg and remaining ingredients. Roll into balls. Place on greased cookie sheet. Flatten cookies (the floured baking powder lid works well). Flatten the cookies some more with a floured fork to give them a waffle appearance. The flatter you can make your cookie without breaking it the better. Bake at 350°F. for about 10 minutes.

Filling:

½	cup butter	1	teaspoon cinnamon
½	cup brown sugar	¼	cup syrup

Mix the filling ingredients in a saucepan and heat and stir until the brown sugar is dissolved. Cool and spread the filling between two cookies.

Lena Redekopp, McMahon

Perfect Pie Crust

2½	cups flour	½	teaspoon salt
½	pound lard	½	cup 7-Up, or as needed

Mix flour and salt, and cut in lard. Add 7-Up gradually, kneading until well blended.

Makes one double 9 inch pie crust.

Cindy Chaykowski, Regina

Mediwnyk (Honey Cake)

4	tablespoons butter	4	cups flour
12	tablespoons white sugar	1	teaspoon baking soda
2	cups melted honey	1	teaspoon allspice
4	eggs	1	cup chopped dates
1	package yeast	½	cup chopped walnuts
½	cup lukewarm water		

Preheat oven to 325°F. Grease a 9 x 13 inch pan or 2 or 3 loaf pans.

Cream butter and sugar well. Add melted honey and 1 egg at a time, beating well after each addition. Dissolve yeast in the lukewarm water. Let stand for 5 minutes, then stir into sugar mixture.

Mix together flour, baking soda and allspice. Add about a quarter at a time, mixing well each time. Finally stir in dates and nuts. Pour into pan or pans and bake for 1 hour.

This cake is best after 2 or 3 days. *NOTE: When cooled, wrap well in plastic wrap or keep in sealed container in a cool place.*

Lennie Pruden, Nipawin

Coconut Butterscotch Cake

2	eggs	½	teaspoon salt
1	cup white sugar	½	cup milk
1	cup flour	2	tablespoons butter
1	teaspoon baking powder		

Beat eggs and add sugar; beat again. Add flour, baking powder and salt. Heat milk to boiling point and add butter. Add to first mixture. Pour batter into a 9 inch square pan and bake for 30 minutes at 350°F.

Topping:

3   tablespoons butter
6   tablespoons brown sugar
3   tablespoons cream
1   cup coconut

Combine the butter, brown sugar and cream in a saucepan and boil 2 minutes. Pour over cake and sprinkle with 1 cup coconut. Return to oven long enough to brown.

Beverly Klimchuk, Saskatoon
Lois Olson, Regina

Pineapple Chocolate Cheesecake

1   box crushed chocolate wafers
5   tablespoons melted butter
1   8 ounce package cream cheese, softened
1   cup icing sugar
2   envelopes dessert topping
1   19 ounce can crushed pineapple, drained

Mix together the chocolate wafers and melted butter. Press into a 9 x 13 inch baking pan, reserving ¼ cup for topping.

Whip the cream cheese and add icing sugar; beat until smooth. Prepare the dessert topping according to package instructions. Mix this whipped cream and the pineapple into the cream cheese mixture. Pour over the wafer base. Sprinkle with remaining wafer crumbs.

This must be refrigerated for 6 hours or frozen for 2 hours. Let stand 10 minutes before serving. *An excellent dessert to store in the freezer for unexpected guests.*

Sharon Nohlgren, Regina

Flaky Pastry

5½ cups flour
2 teaspoons salt
1 pound lard
1 tablespoon vinegar
1 egg, slightly beaten
water

Combine flour and salt. Cut in lard until mixture resembles coarse meal with a few larger pieces. In a measuring cup, combine vinegar and egg. Add water to make one cup. Gradually stir liquid into lard mixture, adding the full cup of liquid. Use a fork to work the mixture together. Gather into a ball and pat until well mixed. *The pastry can be used immediately or wrapped and placed in the fridge or freezer until needed. Recipe can be halved successfully.*

Yields enough pastry for three 9 inch double crust pies or 6 dozen tarts.

Ellen Peterson, Regina
Hilary Davies, Regina

Grasshopper Pie

1 pound chocolate oreo cookies
¼ cup melted butter
1 package white marshmallows
1 cup milk
1 pint cream, whipped
6 tablespoons green creme de menthe

Separate cookies, and mix centres in with the crumbs. Crush until fine and add melted butter. Mix well. Flatten this mixture in a 9 x 13 inch pan, or in two pie plates. Save some crumbs for the top.

In the top of a double boiler, melt marshmallows in milk. Set aside to cool until syrupy. When cool, whip the cream and add to marshmallows. Fold in creme de menthe. Pour over crust. Add crumb topping and refrigerate overnight, or freeze if desired.

Debra Dumontel, Regina
Dianne McEwan, Regina

Blueberry Banana Pie

2 baked pie shells
Bananas, about 5 medium
2 envelopes dessert topping
1 cup milk
1 teaspoon vanilla
1 8 ounce package cream cheese
juice of 1 lemon
1 cup sugar
1 19 ounce can blueberry pie filling

Slice bananas into the pie shells. Beat the dessert topping with milk and vanilla, according to package directions.

Cream together the cream cheese, lemon juice and sugar, and combine with the whipped mixture. Place this on top of the bananas.

Top with chilled blueberry pie filling or other flavor if desired.

Wanda Falkowsky, Regina

Cranberry Pie

3 cups cranberries
¾ cup white sugar
¾ cup chopped nuts
3 eggs beaten
1½ cups white sugar
1½ cups flour
¾ teaspoon salt
¾ cup melted margarine
⅜ cup melted shortening or salad oil

Mix together the cranberries, ¾ cup sugar, and nuts. Divide evenly into 2 greased pie plates.

Make a batter by mixing together the eggs, 1½ cups sugar, flour, salt, margarine and shortening. Pour the batter over the cranberry mixtures in the pie plates. Bake for 1 hour at 325°F. *Good served with ice cream.*

Muriel Barsaloux, Saskatoon

French Apple Pie

1	single pie crust, unbaked	¼	cup white sugar
¾	pound apples, peeled and sliced thin	½	cup firmly packed brown sugar
2	tablespoons lemon juice	2	tablespoons flour
¼	cup raisins, rinsed	2	tablespoons butter
¾	teaspoon cinnamon	¼	cup chopped pecans
¼	teaspoon nutmeg		Brandy Hard Sauce

Line a 9 inch pie plate with pastry. Fill with apples and sprinkle with lemon juice and raisins. Combine cinnamon, nutmeg and white sugar in a bowl. Sprinkle over apples. Blend brown sugar, flour and butter in a small bowl until crumbly. Mix in pecans and sprinkle over filling. Bake at 400°F., covered with tin foil, for 45 to 50 minutes.

Brandy Hard Sauce:

½	cup butter, softened	1	tablespoon boiling water
1½	cups icing sugar	1	teaspoon brandy

Beat butter and icing sugar. Add water. Beat in brandy and serve with the pie.

Cheryl Haw, Saskatoon

Sour Cream Raisin Pie

1	9 inch pie shell, baked	¾	cup sugar
1	cup raisins	¾	cup sour cream
1	cup water	½	teaspoon cinnamon
2	egg yolks	1	teapoon baking soda

Meringue:

2	egg whites	4	tablespoons sugar

Cook the raisins in the water 20 minutes in a large saucepan.

Beat egg yolks; add sugar, cream and cinnamon. Add this mixture to raisins and let come to a boil. Add the baking soda, stir well, and then pour into a baked pie shell. Top with meringue.

To obtain meringue, beat the egg whites to a froth and slowly add sugar while continuing to beat until stiff peaks are formed. Top the pie and brown 10 minutes in a 375°F. oven.

Wendy Hudon, Saskatoon
Lynne Thomas, Regina

Mud Pie

1¼ cups ground chocolate wafer crumbs	2 tablespoons chocolate syrup or chocolate liqueur
½ cup butter or margarine	½ cup whipping cream
1 quart vanilla ice cream	Shaved chocolate
2 tablespoons instant coffee	

Melt butter in pan, and add to chocolate wafer crumbs. Mix. Press into a 9 inch pie plate and pack around sides and bottom.

Soften the ice cream and mix in the instant coffee, until well blended. Pack into crumb shell. Sprinkle chocolate syrup on top of ice cream.

Whip cream until peaks form. Cover pie with the whipped cream and sprinkle with shaved chocolate. Freeze. Keep at room temperature 15 minutes before serving.

Serves 6.

Lucia Harold, Regina

Graham Wafers (1902)

This is an eighty-year-old recipe from Mormon friends in Alberquerque. The wafers are moist and smell delicious. They keep well if kept in a cool place in a closed container.

½	cup butter or margarine	2	tablespoons warm water
¼	cup sugar (or a little less than ¼ cup honey)	½	cup milk
1	egg, slightly beaten	2½ to 2¾	cups whole wheat flour
1	teaspoon baking soda		

Preheat oven to 350°F. Cream together butter and sugar. Add egg. Dissolve baking soda into water and combine with milk. Add to creamed mixture. Blend in flour gradually.

Roll (or press with hands) dough out on well-floured surface to ⅛ inch thickness. Cut into rectangles 3 x 1½ inches. Place on greased cookie sheet. Bake at 350°F. for 15 minutes until golden. Makes approximately 50 wafers. *NOTE: For sweeter cookies, sprinkle sugar or sugar/cinnamon mixture on wafers before baking.*

Ruth Griffiths, Prince Albert

Rhubarb Sherbet

6	cups rhubarb, cut into 1 inch pieces	2	cups white sugar
2	cups water	½	teaspoon salt
1	envelope unflavored gelatin		few drops red food coloring (optional)
¼	cup cold water	1	egg white
		2	tablespoons white sugar

Combine rhubarb and 2 cups water in a saucepan. Cover and cook until tender.

Soak gelatin in ¼ cup cold water for 5 minutes. Add soaked gelatin to hot rhubarb and stir. Add 2 cups sugar, salt and food coloring. Mix well.

Pour into freezer trays and freeze to a firm mush.

Beat egg white until foamy; add 2 tablespoons sugar gradually, beating until stiff. Turn rhubarb mixture into a chilled bowl, beat 1 minute, then fold in egg white.

Quickly return to freezer trays or plastic containers and freeze until firm.

Yield 8 servings.

Eleanor Robertson, Maidstone

Coffee Tortoni

Recommend a double recipe!

1	cup whipping cream, whipped	1	egg white
¼	cup sugar	1	tablespoon sugar
½	teaspoon instant coffee	¼	cup chopped almonds
1	teaspoon vanilla	¼	cup crumbled toasted coconut
few drops almond extract			

Fold the ¼ cup sugar, coffee, vanilla and almond extract into the whipped cream.

Beat the egg white until it peaks, and add 1 tablespoon sugar. Combine chopped almonds and toasted coconut and add half of it to the beaten egg white. Fold egg white mixture into whipped cream mixture. Spoon into 8 paper cups in muffin tin. Sprinkle remainder of nut-coconut mixture on top. Freeze. Put in refrigerator 1 hour before serving. *Top each with a cherry.*

Mary Grebinsky, Regina

Apple Cheese Pizza

2¼ cups flour
¾ teaspoon baking powder
½ teaspoon salt
⅔ cup chilled shortening
1⅓ cups Cheddar cheese, shredded
¼ to ⅓ cup cold water
5 to 7 tart medium apples
½ cup white sugar
¼ teaspoon nutmeg
1 teaspoon cinnamon
2 teaspoons lemon juice
½ cup brown sugar
½ cup butter
¾ cup flour

Mix together the 2¼ cups flour, baking powder and salt. Cut in the shortening until crumbly. Add cheese and mix well. Sprinkle the dough with water and blend lightly. Roll or press the dough into a pizza pan, leaving a ridge around the edges.

Peel and thinly slice the apples onto the pastry. Combine sugar, nutmeg, cinnamon and lemon juice and sprinkle over apples.

Rub together the brown sugar, butter and ¾ cup of flour and sprinkle on top of pizza.

Bake for 30 minutes at 350°F. *Serve with ice cream or whipped cream.*

Dawna Brown, Hawarden

Chocolate Dessert

1 cup flour
½ cup butter
1 teaspoon sugar
½ cup chopped nuts (brazil or almonds)
2 pint containers of prepared whipped topping
1 cup icing sugar
1 8 ounce package cream cheese
1 3 ounce package instant vanilla pudding
1 3 ounce package instant chocolate pudding
3 cups milk
1 square semi-sweet chocolate

Mix together flour, butter, sugar and nuts. Press into a 9 x 13 inch pan and bake at 350°F. for 15 minutes. Cool.

Beat together one container whipped topping, icing sugar and cream cheese. Pour over the bottom layer.

Beat together the vanilla and chocolate puddings with the milk and pour over the cream cheese layer. On top of this, pour the other container of whipped topping.

Shave the square of semi-sweet chocolate over top. Store in the refrigerator. *This dessert will keep for several days.*

Elsie Taves, Regina

Impossible Pie

4	eggs	1	cup white sugar
½	cup margarine	1	cup coconut
½	cup flour	2	teaspoons vanilla
2	cups milk	¼	teaspoon nutmeg

Blend eggs, margarine, flour, milk, sugar, coconut, vanilla and nutmeg in a blender. Pour into a greased 10 inch pie pan, and bake at 350°F. for one hour. *Flour settles to form a crust. The coconut forms a topping, and the centre is an egg custard filling.*

Edith Shier, Saskatoon
Florence Berjian, Regina
Shelley Hahn, Swift Current
Doris Bell, Regina

Cheese Crumble Pie

1	cup grated Cheddar cheese	1	teaspoon baking powder
½	cup margarine	4	cups chopped apples, peeled
1½	cups flour	⅔	cup sugar
2	tablespoons sugar	½	teaspoon cinnamon

To make the pastry, cream cheese and margarine. Add flour, sugar, and baking powder. Press one-half of this mixture into a greased 9 inch pie plate.

Make filling by combining apples, ⅔ cup sugar and cinnamon. Spread over base and top with remaining pastry mixture. Bake at 375°F. for 30 to 40 minutes.

Norma Vik, Saskatoon

Cherry Cho Cho

1½	cups crushed graham wafers	4	cups miniature marshmallows
⅓	cup butter, melted	1	19 ounce can cherry pie filling
3	tablespoons icing sugar		
½	pint whipping cream		

Mix graham wafer crumbs, melted butter and icing sugar. Take out 2 tablespoons for topping. Press into a 9 x 9 inch pan. Chill for at least 1 hour.

Whip cream and fold in marshmallows. Put ½ of this mixture on chilled crust. Gently top with cherry pie filling. Cover with rest of cream mixture. Sprinkle with crumbs. Cover and refrigerate. *May be made a day ahead.*

Wanda Falkowsky, Regina

Tapioca Pudding

¾ cup tapioca
½ to ¾ cup water
2 cups milk, divided
½ cup white sugar
1 egg
1 tablespoon butter
dash of vanilla

Wash tapioca in water, and drain. Soak the washed tapioca in 1 cup of the milk for about 6 to 8 hours.

Put 1 cup of the milk in a pot. Heat, then add tapioca and milk mixture. Add sugar. Cook slowly until thick. Beat egg and add to above mixture after it has cooled slightly.

Add butter and a dash of vanilla and pour into a greased baking dish. Bake at 325°F. for 45 minutes or until golden brown on top.

Makes 6 to 8 servings.

Patricia Gutfriend, Regina

Old-Fashioned Bread Pudding

2 eggs
½ cup white sugar
1 13 ounce can evaporated milk
1 cup water
1 teaspoon vanilla extract
5 slices buttered white bread, cut into cubes
½ cup raisins
cinnamon

Beat eggs with sugar. Add milk, water, and vanilla and mix. Fold in bread cubes and raisins. Pour into a greased 1½ to 2 quart casserole dish, and sprinkle with cinnamon. Bake at 375°F. for 45 minutes, uncovered.

Makes 6 to 8 servings.

Christina Patoine, Regina

Carrot Pudding

½ cup butter or lard
1 cup brown sugar
1 cup grated carrot
1 cup grated potato
1 cup grated apple
1 cup raisins
½ cup currants
¼ cup citron

¼ cup chopped nuts
½ cup flour
1 teaspoon baking soda
1 teaspoon cinnamon
½ teaspoon cloves
½ teaspoon salt
1 cup bread crumbs

Cream butter until light. Gradually cream in the brown sugar and beat until the mixture is light and fluffy.

Peel carrots, potatoes, and apples; then grate them and measure a cup of each. Add these to the creamed mixture, mixing well.

Wash and drain the raisins and currants and dry thoroughly. Cut the raisins if desired and chop the citron finely. Add the fruit and nuts to the original mixture.

Sift the flour with the baking soda, cinnamon, cloves and salt, then stir in the bread crumbs. Add this to the original mixture and stir thoroughly. Fill pudding bowls ⅔ full, cover with wax paper, tie on with a string, and wrap in a tea towel. Use the corners of the tea towel to tie knots above the bowl for easy removal from the water. Place on a rack in a canner or large kettle, and fill with water half way up the bowls.

Steam the pudding for 3 hours.

Alternately, the pudding may be put into pint sealers, with a rubber ring, glass top and metal ring. Steam for 3 hours with the metal cap loosened, then tighten and seal, before cooling. Pudding will keep for months.

Pudding Sauce:

1 cup white sugar
4½ tablespoons flour
pinch of salt

3 cups boiling water
¼ pound butter
3 teaspoons vanilla

Mix together the sugar, flour and salt. Add boiling water, stirring all the while. Bring to a boil and boil for 5 minutes, or until slightly thickened. Remove from stove and add butter and vanilla.

Serve over warm pudding.

Marilyn Nelson, Griffin

Plum Crumb Dessert

4	cups quartered, pitted red plums	1	cup brown sugar
¼	cup granulated sugar	¼	teaspoon salt
2	tablespoons lemon juice	¼	teaspoon mace or nutmeg
1¼	cups stirred, but unsifted flour (or 1 cup flour and ¼ cup rolled oats)	½	cup butter
		½	pint fresh dairy sour cream

Wash, cut into quarters and pit the plums. (About 24 medium sized plums weighing two pounds). Arrange plums in medium-sized baking dish and sprinkle with the ¼ cup granulated sugar and the lemon juice.

Combine flour (or flour and rolled oats), brown sugar, salt and spice. Cut the butter into this mixture using a pastry blender or with the finger tips. Take care not to mix it too well or it will be oily. Pat this crumb mixture evenly over the plums. Stand the prepared dish on centre shelf of oven. NOTE: If baked on bottom shelf of oven, the plums cook too quickly and boil up over the crumb mixture and prevent browning. Bake at 375°F. for about 30 to 40 minutes, depending on size of plums. *This dessert is best served at the table slightly warm with the fresh dairy sour cream ladled, ice-cold, over it.*

Olga Lange, Regina

Pfeffernusse (Pepper Nuts)

A favorite German Christmas Cookie

1½ cups strained honey	1 teaspoon nutmeg
¼ cup shortening	1 teaspoon allspice
1 egg	¾ teaspoon ground cardamom seed
4 cups sifted flour	
1 teaspoon salt	½ teaspoon black pepper
1 teaspoon baking soda	¼ teaspoon finely crushed anise seed
1 teaspoon baking powder	

Heat honey (do not boil) in a 4 quart saucepan. Add shortening and cool. Beat in egg.

Sift dry ingredients together; gradually stir into the honey mixture. Knead dough slightly in bowl or on a board. Let dough stand 30 to 40 minutes.

Shape dough into 1 inch balls and place on lightly greased baking sheets. Bake in a preheated 350°F. oven for 13 to 15 minutes.

Yield: 96 to 108 cookies.

Pfeffernusse Frosting:

2 unbeaten egg whites	¼ teaspoon ground cardamom seed
1 tablespoon strained honey	2 cups icing sugar
½ teaspoon finely crumbled anise seed	

Combine egg whites, honey and spices in a 1 quart bowl. Gradually beat in icing sugar, using a beater or mixer. Place 12 to 14 Pfeffernusse in a bowl with 2 tablespoons of frosting. Stir gently to coat all sides. Place on a wire rack for frosting to harden. Store in a tightly closed container.

Hertha Pfeifer, Regina

Bavarian Apple Torte

½	cup margarine	½	teaspoon vanilla
⅓	cup sugar	⅓	cup sugar
¼	teaspoon vanilla	½	teaspoon or more cinnamon
1	cup flour		
1	8 ounce package cream cheese	4	cups peeled and sliced apples
¼	cup sugar	¼	cup flaked almonds
1	egg		

Cream margarine, sugar and vanilla. Blend in flour. Spread on the bottom and sides of a 9 inch spring form pan; do not pack too hard.

Combine softened cream cheese and sugar. Mix well. Blend in egg and vanilla. Pour onto pastry.

Combine sugar and cinnamon. Toss apples in this sugar mixture before spooning them over the cheese mixture. Sprinkle with almonds and bake at 450°F. for 10 minutes. Reduce heat to 400°F. and bake 25 minutes more.

Loosen torte from rim. Cool before removing rim of pan.

Carol Bonli, Melfort

Soft Icing

1	cup milk	1	cup white sugar
2	tablespoons cornstarch	1	teaspoon vanilla
1	cup soft butter		

Heat the milk and cornstarch over medium heat until thick, stirring constantly. Beat the soft butter and sugar until it's like whipped cream. Add the vanilla and cooled milk mixture. Beat for a few minutes and add coloring if desired. *This icing is not too sweet and it is plenty to ice a large layer or angel food cake.*

Debbie Ulmer, Wilcox

German Strudel

Dough:

4 cups flour	dash of salt
2 cups warm water	soft butter

Mix flour, water and salt together to make a soft dough. Place the dough on counter, and knead until nice and smooth (dough will be a little sticky to fingers but soft). The more you throw around the dough, the better will be the strudel pastry! Put in a buttered dish, butter top of dough, cover and set in a very warm place for at least two hours or overnight. In this time prepare the filling.

To roll the dough, place a cotton cloth on a 36 x 72 inch table and flour very lightly. Working quickly, pull dough until it is paper thin and covers the table and over hangs the sides. Remove and discard the excess thick dough along edges. Add your choices of filling as instructed below. Using the cloth fold up the hanging ends and sides to make a double thickness of dough. Put more filling on these layers.

Now, working from both sides of the table, take the sides of the cloth and roll strudel up like a jelly roll to the center. You will now have two rolls meeting in the middle of the table. Into greased pans, place the rolls, which have been cut to fit the pans, and brush with butter or cream. Bake about 1 hour at 350°F. Cut in squares to serve.

Fillings:

1.

½ cup melted butter	2 tablespoons cinnamon
½ box of apples	½ cup bread crumbs (optional)
3 cups white sugar	

Peel and slice the apples. Spread the melted butter over the stretched dough and add the apple slices. Mix the sugar with the cinnamon and add to the table. Add the bread crumbs, if used.

2.

½	cup melted butter	2	cups sour cream
1	pound poppy seeds	2½	to 3 cups white sugar
6	eggs, well beaten	2	tablespoons cinnamon

Spread butter over the stretched dough and add poppy. Beat cream with beaten eggs a little. Mix the sugar and cinnamon, and add with cream mixture to the table.

Brenda Martin, Lumsden

Kuehen (Kuchka)

Kuehen (pronounced kooken) literally means "cream squares". It is an old family recipe brought by my greatgrandmother from Germany more than 60 years ago. It is a special family favorite in the early spring when fresh farm cream is abundant.

4	cups flour	3	eggs
1	cup sugar	1	cup cream (or canned milk)
1	teaspoon salt		
2½	teaspoons baking powder		milk as needed
½	cup lard		brown or white sugar
½	cup margarine		cinnamon

Combine dry ingredients. Cut in lard and margarine. Add eggs and cream. Add enough additional milk to form a medium soft dough if kneaded. Roll out to approximately ⅓ inch thickness. (It must be quite thick). Place in 9 x 13 inch pans, pressing a ½ inch border around the edge. Prick the pastry with a fork as it does form large air pockets.

Pour more sweet cream over pastry. Sprinkle with brown or white sugar and then with cinnamon. Bake at 350°F. until pastry is golden brown. Cool and cut in squares.

Joanne Jansen, Nipawin

Oh-So-Good Cookies

½	cup butter	½	teaspoon baking soda
½	cup brown sugar, packed	¼	teaspoon salt
½	cup granulated sugar	1	cup rolled oats
1	egg	1	cup chocolate chips
1	teaspoon vanilla	½	cup chopped nuts
⅔	cup whole wheat flour (or white flour)	½	cup raisins

Cream butter, sugars, egg, and vanilla together until fluffy. Stir in flour, soda and salt. Blend well. Stir in rolled oats, chocolate chips, nuts and raisins. Drop by teaspoonful onto greased baking sheets, allowing space for spreading. Press flat with a floured fork. Bake at 375°F. for 8 to 10 minutes. Carefully lift off pan. Cool.

Yields about 3 dozen.

Gwen Veikle, Cut Knife

Banana Slice

	whole graham wafers		about 4 bananas
½	cup butter, softened but not melted	½	pint whipping cream
		2	tablespoons white sugar
1½	cups icing sugar	¼	cup crushed nuts
2	eggs, well-beaten		

Place a layer of graham wafers in a 9 x 13 inch pan. Beat together the butter and icing sugar, then add well-beaten eggs. Spread over wafers. Put layers of sliced bananas over egg mixture. Whip the cream and sweeten it with the sugar. Spread whipped cream over bananas and sprinkle with crushed nuts. Keep refrigerated overnight before serving.

Patricia Brown, Swift Current

Sand Cookies

1	cup margarine	1	teaspoon baking soda
1	cup white sugar	1	teaspoon salt
1	cup brown sugar	1	teaspoon cream of tartar
1	egg	2	cups rice krispies or
1	cup oil		2 cups coconut
2	teaspoons vanilla	1	cup oatmeal
4	cups flour		

Cream butter and sugar thoroughly; add egg, oil and vanilla and beat well. Sift together the flour, baking soda, salt and cream of tartar and add to first mixture. Add rice krispies or coconut and oatmeal. The mixture will be dry and crumbly. Roll into balls and place on a greased cookie sheet. Flatten each with a fork. Bake at 375°F. about 10 minutes, or until a light golden brown in color.

Sheena Wirges, Coderre

Ginger Sparklers

¾	cup margarine	1	teaspoon baking soda
1	cup white sugar	½	teaspoon salt
1	egg	1	teaspoon cinnamon
¼	cup molasses	½	teaspoon cloves
2	cups flour	½	teaspoon ginger

Cream margarine and sugar. Add egg and molasses. Beat well. Stir in dry ingredients. Roll in balls and coat with sugar. Place on greased baking sheet and flatten with thumb. Leave lots of room between each cookie. Bake at 350°F. for 10 minutes.

Makes 5 dozen.

Wendy Wuschke, Regina.
Debbie Mything, Climax.
Maureen Materi, Lipton.

Butterscotch Jumbles

½ cup shortening
1½ cups brown sugar
2 eggs
1 cup sour cream
1 teaspoon vanilla
2¾ cups flour
½ teaspoon baking soda
1 teaspoon salt

Cream shortening with sugar, and mix in eggs. Stir in sour cream and vanilla. Blend in flour, soda and salt. Chill dough if soft. Heat oven to 375°F. Drop by tablespoon 2 inches apart on a greased baking sheet. Bake about 10 minutes. Spread cookies with Browned Butter Glaze.

Browned Butter Glaze:

½ cup butter
2 cups icing sugar
1 teaspoon vanilla
2 to 4 tablespoons hot water

Melt butter until golden brown. Blend in icing sugar and vanilla. Stir in hot water until it spreads smoothly.

Patricia Gutfriend, Regina

Cheese Cookies

1 cup white flour
2 teaspoons baking powder
⅛ teaspoon salt
½ cup butter
1 cup grated cheese (Cheddar sharp or Cracker Barrel old)
½ cup water

Sift together flour, baking powder and salt. Cut in butter with pastry blender. Grate cheese with a coarse grater. Add cheese and mix. Turn oven to 450°F. Add water and mix. Grease cookie sheet. Drop mixture onto cookie sheet by teaspoons. Bake 12 minutes. *NOTE: Smell of them through the house is nice. You can mix together all but baking powder and water; store in fridge and add baking powder and water just before baking.*

Sandra Dowie, Regina

Trifle

2	cups cake cubes (white cake or sponge)	1	3 ounce package cherry flavored jello
¼	cup sherry, brandy or rum (or ⅓ cup juice)	2	cups soft custard
2	cups drained sweetened fruit (fruit cocktail, bananas, orange segments, or any other)	1	cup whipping cream
		2	tablespoons white sugar

In a glass bowl or fruit serving bowl, place cake cubes. Pour liquor (or juice) over the cake. Allow to soak in and toss cubes gently.

Prepare jello powder as directed on the package. Allow jello to thicken, and stir in the drained fruit. Pour onto cake and allow to set.

Make your favorite custard recipe, or use the canned custard powder and prepare as directed. Spread the custard on top of the jello layer. Allow to set. Whip the whipping cream until stiff, adding the sugar gradually until stiff peaks form. Spread on top of the custard layer. *Garnish with fruit pieces or toasted almonds, if desired.*

Emma Wadsworth, Moose Jaw

Bachelor Buttons

¾ cup butter or margarine
1½ cups brown sugar
2 eggs, slightly beaten
2 cups all-purpose flour
1 teaspoon baking soda
pinch of salt
strawberry jam

Cream butter and sugar; add eggs and beat with a fork. Add dry ingredients and mix well with hand mixing.

Drop dough one-half teaspoon at a time onto a greased cookie sheet and press down with a fork. Bake 8 to 10 minutes at 375°F. Cookies will spread quite flat when baking. Watch closely, as they burn easily.

Cool, and then spread 1 teaspoon of strawberry jam on a cookie and sandwich it together with another cookie of approximately the same size. Continue with remainder of cookies until all are "sandwiched". *Store cookies in a tightly closed container. As they sit, the jam will moisten the cookie, making it very soft and yummy!*

Christina Patoine, Regina

Pumpkin Ice Cream Squares

A good dessert replacement for the traditional pumpkin pie.

1½ cups graham wafer crumbs
¼ cup sugar
¼ cup melted butter
2 cups pumpkin
½ cup brown sugar
½ teaspoon salt
1 teaspoon cinnamon
¼ teaspoon ginger
¼ teaspoon cloves
1 quart vanilla ice cream, softened
whipped cream

Mix crumbs with sugar and butter; press into a 9 inch square pan. Combine pumpkin, brown sugar, salt and spices. Fold in ice cream. Pour mixture over crumbs. Cover and freeze until firm.

Cut into squares about 20 minutes before serving. Top with whipped cream.

Adeline Wilson, Archerwill

Banana Split Dessert

¼	cup melted margarine	2	bananas
2	cups graham wafer crumbs	1	14 ounce can crushed pineapple
½	cup melted margarine	1	envelope dessert topping
1	egg, beaten		Nuts to garnish
2	cups icing sugar		

Mix well together the ¼ cup margarine and graham wafer crumbs. Pat into a 9 x 9 inch pan.

Combine the ½ cup margarine, egg and icing sugar. Spread over crumb bottom.

Over this, slice the bananas, and top with crushed pineapple, which has been very well drained.

Prepare the dessert topping as directed on the package, and spread over the pineapple. Top with nuts. Refrigerate 3 hours.

Beryl Erickson, Estevan

Danish Apple Bars

Pastry:

2½ cups flour
1 teaspoon salt
1 cup shortening
1 egg yolk, slightly beaten

⅔ cup milk (enough to make ⅔ cup with egg yolk)

Filling:

1 cup cornflakes
4 medium apples
1 teaspoon cinnamon

1 cup sugar
1 egg white

For pastry, sift together flour and salt; add shortening and cut like coarse meal. Slowly add egg yolk to milk; add to first mixture and mix. Divide dough in half and roll into rectangle large enough for a cookie sheet, bringing pastry up sides.

Preheat oven to 400°F.

Sprinkle the cornflakes onto pastry. Peel and slice the apples over cornflakes. Combine the cinnamon and sugar and sprinkle over the apples. Roll the other half of dough and place over apples. Moisten edges of pastry with milk and pinch layers together. Beat the egg white until stiff, and brush evenly over top crust. Bake for 1 hour.

Glaze:

1 cup icing sugar
1 tablespoon (or more) water

1 teaspoon vanilla

Mix above ingredients together and ice while still warm.

Shirley Birtles, Lockwood

Pineapple Slices

2 cups flour	2 egg yolks
2 tablespoons white sugar	¾ cup chopped marachino cherries
1 cup butter	
pinch of salt	2 egg whites
1 15 ounce can crushed pineapple, undrained	2 tablespoons sugar
	¼ teaspoon almond flavoring
¼ cup white sugar	
¼ cup cold water	⅓ cup sweetened, flaked coconut
2 tablespoons cornstarch	

Blend flour, butter, sugar and salt until crumbly. Pat into a 9 x 12 inch pan. Bake in a moderate oven (350°F.) for about 20 minutes or until lightly browned.

Cook pineapple, sugar and cornstarch mixed with the cold water until thick. Stir often. Cool and add slightly beaten egg yolks and cherries. Spread over baked base.

Beat egg whites with sugar until stiff. Add flavoring. Spread over filling and sprinkle with coconut. Bake in moderate oven until meringue is golden. Cut into squares.

Cindy Quist, Regina
Debbie Mything, Climax
Pearl Fahlman, Fillmore

Ricketty Uncles

½ cup butter	1 teaspoon vanilla
1 cup brown sugar	2 cups rolled oats
½ teaspoon baking soda	

Heat butter and sugar but do not boil. Add soda and stir until the mixture has the consistency of creamed honey. Remove from heat and add vanilla and oatmeal. Press into ungreased pan and bake at 375°F. for 10 to 15 minutes. Cut into squares while warm.

Tammy MacDonald, Regina

Peanut Butter Slice

1 cup peanut butter
½ cup brown sugar
½ cup corn syrup

2 cups corn flakes
1 cup rice krispies

Mix the peanut butter, brown sugar and corn syrup in the top of a double boiler. Heat until it all blends together. Cool slightly and add the corn flakes and rice krispies. Mix thoroughly. Press into a 9 x 9 inch, greased cake pan. Cool.

Icing:

1 cup brown sugar
3 tablespoons cream
2 tablespoons butter

1 teaspoon vanilla
pinch of salt

Blend sugar, cream, butter, vanilla and salt together in a saucepan over medium heat. Boil for 1 minute, stirring constantly. Beat slightly with spoon before spreading. Spread onto cake while icing is still hot.

Darlene McHardy, Regina
Florence Dugan, Melfort

Sweet Marie Bars

1 tablespoon butter
½ cup brown sugar
½ cup syrup
½ cup peanut butter

1 cup Spanish peanuts
2 cups rice krispies
1 teaspoon vanilla
chocolate icing

Mix the butter, brown sugar and syrup together in a saucepan and heat to boiling. Add the peanut butter, peanuts, rice krispies and vanilla. Mix until well blended. Spread in an 8 x 8 inch greased pan. Frost with your favorite chocolate icing. Cool thoroughly, and slice into squares.

Barb Wiebe, Swift Current

Tweedies

½ cup margarine
⅔ cup sugar
1½ cups flour
2 teaspoons baking powder
½ teaspoon salt

1 cup milk
2 squares semi-sweet chocolate, grated
1 teaspoon vanilla
2 egg whites, beaten stiff

Cream margarine and sugar. Add dry ingredients alternately with milk. Then add grated chocolate and vanilla. Fold in egg whites.

Bake for 30 minutes at 350°F. in a 9 x 13 x 2 inch pan. Cool.

Topping:

⅓ cup margarine, softened
2 cups icing sugar

2 egg yolks
1 teaspoon vanilla

Mix all ingredients and spread on cooled cake.

Icing:

1 tablespoon salad oil
2 squares semi-sweet chocolate

⅓ cup crushed walnuts

Melt chocolate with oil in the top of a double boiler. Pour in ribbon effect over topping on cake. Sprinkle with crushed walnuts. *This cake must be kept in a cool place as the chocolate in the base tends to melt easily.*

Joanne Jansen, Nipawin
Diana Starosta, Regina

Apple Cinnamon Puffs

4	to 6 medium apples, peeled and cored	¼	cup shortening
1	cup white sugar	¾	cup milk
1	cup water	2	tablespoons butter, melted
1½	cups flour	½	teaspoon cinnamon
2	teaspoons baking powder	2	tablespoons sugar
½	teaspoon salt		

Slice the peeled apples into a shallow pan. Boil sugar and water for about 5 minutes and pour over apples.

Sift together the flour, baking powder and salt. Mix with the shortening and add milk to make a soft dough. Drop dough with a teaspoon on top of apples. Make an indentation with finger in each dough and fill with a mixture of butter, cinnamon and 2 tablespoons sugar.

Bake 30 minutes at 375°F.

Anita Veikle, Cut Knife

Buttertarts

3	tablespoons margarine		pinch of salt
⅔	cup brown sugar	½	cup raisins, washed in hot water
2	eggs, slightly beaten		
¾	cup corn syrup	½	cup chopped nuts (optional)
½	teaspoon vanilla		

Cream together margarine and sugar, then add eggs. Add syrup, vanilla, salt, raisins and nuts. Beat together with a fork. Fill pastry cups ⅔ full with mixture. Place in 375°F. oven on middle rack for 15 to 20 minutes, or until bubbling.

Makes 2 dozen tarts.

Ellen Peterson, Regina

Fudgy Oatmeal Brownies

1	cup flour	2	teaspoons vanilla
¾	cup rolled oats	1	cup oil
¼	cup wheat germ	4	eggs
1	teaspoon salt	½	cup cold water
1½	cups white sugar	½	cup chopped nuts
½	cup cocoa		

Mix dry ingredients together in a beater bowl. Add oil, vanilla, eggs and cold water. Beat on low until smooth, but do not over beat. Stir in chopped nuts.

Bake in a 9 x 13 greased pan at 350°F. for 30 minutes. If using a glass pan, use 325°F. for 30 minutes.

Lois Miller, Broadview

Hello Dollies

½	cup butter	1	cup shredded coconut
2	cups graham wafer crumbs	1	cup chopped pecans
1	6 ounce package butterscotch chips	1	can sweetened condensed milk
1	6 ounce package semi-sweet chocolate chips		

Set oven to 325°F. Melt butter in 9 x 13 inch pan. Layer the other ingredients over the butter in the order listed. Do not mix. Bake for 20 minutes. Cool and refrigerate. Cut into squares when cold.

Sandra Dowie, Regina
Tina Ash, Regina
Carole Coulthard, Regina

Jelly Roll

4	egg whites	¾	cup flour
¾	cup white sugar	¾	teaspoon baking powder
4	egg yolks	¼	teaspoon salt
½	teaspoon lemon flavoring		jam

Beat egg whites until stiff but not dry. Gradually add sugar and beat until very stiff.

Beat egg yolks until very thick. Add them to the beaten whites. Add lemon flavoring and mix. Sift together the flour, baking powder and salt and fold into the egg mixture.

Bake on a wax paper lined small cookie sheet at 400°F. for 10 minutes. Turn the cake onto a damp towel and roll. Fill with jam when cool.

Dale Gerhardt, Regina

Peach Crumbly Crust Pie

4	cups sliced peaches	½	cup butter
1	cup flour	½	cup brown sugar
1	cup sugar	¼	teaspoon cinnamon
½	teaspoon salt	¼	teaspoon nutmeg
2	tablespoons lemon juice	1	9 inch pie shell, unbaked

Preheat oven to 450°F. Line a pie plate with uncooked pastry and flute rim.

Combine sliced peaches with ¼ cup flour, sugar and salt. Place in pie shell and sprinkle with lemon juice.

Cream butter and work in the remaining ¾ cup flour, brown sugar, cinnamon and nutmeg until the mixture is crumbly. Spread over peaches.

Bake for 10 minutes at 450°F. Reduce heat to 350°F. and bake for an additional one-half hour.

Linda Travland, Regina

Taster's Choice

Once there was a little girl
Who wanted to be a cook.
The problem was, she couldn't read
A word, much less a book!

She's only four years old, you see
But her goal was then quite set:
She'd bake a pie, her very first,
The best in the land, I'd bet!

She'd watched her Mom whip up a pie
She'd tasted quite a few
So Sally (that's our little girl)
Thought she knew just what to do.

She used natural ground ingredients
She removed the stones — no lies!
She oven-baked it in the sun
Then served her friends mud pies!

Flour Power

**BREADS
BUNS
MUFFINS
LOAVES
PANCAKES**

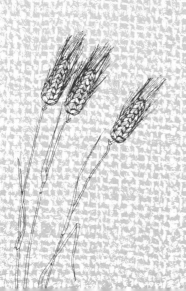
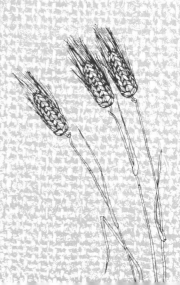

Date & Orange Muffins

1	whole orange	1	teaspoon baking powder
½	cup orange juice	1	teaspoon baking soda
½	cup dates, chopped	¾	cup sugar
1	egg	1	scant teaspoon salt
½	cup margarine	½	cup wheat germ
1½	cups flour		

Cut orange into small pieces, remove seeds, place in blender. Blend till rind is finely ground. Add juice, dates, egg and margarine. Blend until smooth.

Into a bowl, sift flour, baking powder, baking soda, sugar and salt. Add wheat germ to sifted ingredients. Pour orange mixture over dry ingredients and mix.

Bake in buttered muffin tins ⅔ full at 400°F. for 15 minutes.

Makes 1 dozen muffins.

Flo Hook, Regina

Bran Muffins

2	cups of all-bran	2	cups of boiling water
2½	cups white sugar	5	cups flour
4	eggs	8	teaspoons baking soda
1¼	cups oil	2	teaspoons salt
4	cups buttermilk	2	cups raisins, chopped
4	cups bran flakes		dates, or diced apples

Pour the boiling water over the all-bran and set aside to cool.

Beat together the white sugar, eggs, oil, and buttermilk. Add the bran mixture to the beaten mixture and combine with a large mixing spoon. Do not use a beater! Then add the bran flakes, flour, soda, salt and fruit and mix thoroughly with mixing spoon. Put in a covered dish. Refrigerate overnight before using. This recipe can be kept in the fridge for up to 6 weeks, but DO NOT STIR as you use the muffin mix.

Bake at 350°F. for 20 minutes.

Yields 8 dozen muffins.

Maxine Mesenchuk, Lanigan
Dawna Brown, Hawarden
Ruth Griffiths, Prince Albert
Sandra Meister, Moosomin
Kaye Loustel, Regina
Flo Hook, Regina

Pumpkin Muffins

2	eggs	1	teaspoon cinnamon
1¼	cups brown sugar	1	teaspoon baking soda
¾	cup oil	1	teaspoon baking powder
1	cup cooked pumpkin (or canned)	pinch of salt	
		1	cup raisins
1½	cups whole wheat flour		

Beat eggs until light. Add sugar and oil, beating after each addition. Add the pumpkin.

Combine the dry ingredients, then mix into pumpkin mixture, along with raisins.

Bake at 375°F. for approximately 20 minutes.

Yields 2 dozen delicious muffins.

Doreen Chomicki, North Battleford

Wheat Germ Muffins

1¼ cups sifted all-purpose flour	1 egg
4 teaspoons baking powder	⅓ cup salad oil
½ teaspoon salt	1 cup water
¼ cup sugar	¼ teaspoon vanilla
¼ cup skim milk powder	1 cup fresh or frozen drained blueberries (optional)
¾ cup fresh wheat germ	

Sift together the flour, baking powder, salt, sugar and skim milk powder. When sifted, add wheat germ. In beater bowl, beat egg and oil to mix, then add water and vanilla. Add dry ingredients all at once and beat to barely blend. Fold in blueberries, if used.

Grease twelve muffin cups, spoon in batter to ⅞ full. Bake at 400°F. about 15 to 20 minutes.

Doris Bell, Regina
Olga Lange, Regina
Donna Petracek, Langenburg

Cinnamon Muffins

2 cups sifted flour	1 egg
¼ cup white sugar	1 cup milk
4 teaspoons baking powder	¼ cup salad oil
½ teaspoon salt	1 teaspoon cinnamon
1 teaspoon cinnamon	2 tablespoons white sugar

Sift the flour, ¼ cup sugar, baking powder, salt and 1 teaspoon cinnamon into a bowl.

Into another bowl, beat the egg and add the milk and salad oil.

Combine the liquid ingredients with the dry ingredients, mixing just enough to moisten completely.

Spoon into greased muffin pans, filling about ⅔ full.

Combine 1 teaspoon cinnamon and 2 tablespoons white sugar to make the topping and sprinkle over top the batter. Bake at 400°F. for 20 minutes.

Yields 12 muffins.

Laurel Madole, Regina

Apricot and Raisin Quickbread

1	cup dried apricots, cut up	½	cup brown sugar
1	cup seedless raisins	½	cup chopped pecans or walnuts
1	cup sifted all-purpose flour	1	tablespoon grated orange rind
2	teaspoons baking powder	2	eggs
1	teaspoon salt	1	cup orange juice
1	cup whole wheat flour	¼	cup salad oil

Put apricots and raisins in a small saucepan, cover with water, bring to boil and simmer for 5 minutes. Cool, drain off any water that has not been absorbed.

Preheat oven to 350°F. Grease a 9 x 5 x 3 inch loaf pan.

Sift all-purpose flour, baking powder and salt together into a bowl. Add whole wheat flour, sugar, apricots, raisins, nuts and orange rind. Mix well.

Beat eggs, juice and oil together, and add to first mixture. Stir just to blend. Spoon into prepared pan. Bake about 60 minutes, then turn out onto a rack to cool. *Slices best if wrapped well, and kept for a day or two.*

Eleanor Robertson, Maidstone

Oat Muffins

1	cup rolled oats	⅔	cup raisins or chopped dates
1	cup sour milk or buttermilk	1	egg, beaten
1	cup flour	¼	cup butter or margarine, melted
1	teaspoon baking powder		
½	teaspoon baking soda		
½	teaspoon salt		
1	cup packed brown sugar		

Combine rolled oats and milk in a small bowl. Let stand.

Combine flour, baking powder, baking soda, and salt. Stir in brown sugar and raisins. Add beaten egg and butter to oat mixture. Mix well.

Add oat mixture all at once to dry ingredients. Stir just until all ingredients are moistened. Fill well greased muffin cups ⅔ full. Bake at 400°F. for about 20 minutes.

Yields 12 muffins.

Cindy Quist, Regina

Applesauce Muffins

6	cups whole wheat flour	1	tablespoon vanilla, or 1 tablespoon maple flavoring, or 1 tablespoon cinnamon (or a combination)
2	cups all-purpose flour		
2	tablespoons baking soda		
2	tablespoons salt		
4	cups white sugar		
6	medium eggs	1	10 ounce can applesauce
3	cups oil	1	pound chopped dates
6	cups, less 2 tablespoons, milk		

Mix all dry ingredients in a large bowl. Mix all liquid ingredients and add to dry ingredients. Mix together until blended. Use cupcake liners and bake at 400°F.

Makes about 8 dozen muffins.

Margaret Tysowski, Regina

Best Bran Muffins

1	cup whole wheat flour	⅓	cup oil
1	cup natural bran	¾	cup milk (only ½ cup when using honey)
2	tablespoons wheat germ		
¾	cup brown sugar or honey	2	tablespoons yogurt (optional)
1	teaspoon salt	1	teaspoon vanilla
1	teaspoon baking powder	1	cup raisins, currants, dates or nuts
1	egg		

Mix dry ingredients together. Mix egg, oil, milk, yogurt (if used) and vanilla in another bowl. Beat liquid mixture into dry ingredients, but don't over mix. Add the raisins or other fruit or nuts, mixing until just blended.

Fill 12 well greased muffin cups about ⅔ full. Bake at 375°F. for 18 to 20 minutes. Cool on a wire rack. *These are very good when slightly warm. The addition of the yogurt makes the muffins very moist.*

Adeline Wilson, Archerwill

Kahlua Loaf Cake

1	cup pitted dates, chopped	⅔	cup brown sugar
½	cup Kahlua liqueur (or orange juice)	2	tablespoons shortening
		1	egg, slightly beaten
½	cup warm water	2	cups flour
1	teaspoon grated orange peel (cherries)	1	teaspoon baking soda
		1	teaspoon salt
		⅔	cup chopped pecans

Mix together the dates, Kahlua, water and orange peel and let stand.

Beat sugar, shortening and egg together until fluffy. Sift together flour, soda and salt. Add to creamed mixture alternately with date mixture.

Stir in pecans. Turn into greased 9 x 5 x 3 inch loaf pan. Let stand 5 minutes. Then bake in moderate oven, 350°F., for 60 to 70 minutes. Cool on wire rack.

Betty Dobson, Regina

Dutch Apple Streusel Coffee Cake

1½	cups flour	1	egg, beaten
2¼	teaspoons baking powder	¾	cup milk
½	cup sugar	¼	cup melted shortening
½	teaspoon salt	1½	cups chopped apples
½	teaspoon cinnamon	¾	cup raisins

Sift flour, baking powder, sugar, salt and cinnamon together. Add beaten egg, milk and shortening to dry ingredients. Add apples and raisins and mix well.

Put into a well greased 8 inch square pan. Sprinkle topping over top and bake at 400°F. for 25 to 35 minutes, or until done.

Topping:

¼ cup white sugar
2 tablespoons flour
1 tablespoon butter
½ teaspoon cinnamon

Mix topping ingredients until crumbly and sprinkle over batter.

Judy McClelland, Regina

Poppy Seed Coffee Cake

1 cup poppy seeds
1 cup sour cream
½ cup butter
½ cup shortening
1½ cups white sugar

4 egg yolks
2½ cups flour
2 teaspoons baking powder
1 teaspoon baking soda
4 egg whites

½ cup brown sugar
1 tablespoon cocoa

1 teaspoon cinnamon

Preheat oven to 350°F. Grease a bundt or chiffon pan.

Combine poppy seeds with sour cream and let stand for at least 15 minutes.

Combine butter, shortening, sugar and egg yolks in large mixing bowl. Beat at medium speed for 2 minutes. Mix in flour, baking powder, and baking soda alternately with sour cream.

Beat the egg whites until stiff and fold into the above mixture.

To make filling, combine the brown sugar, cocoa and cinnamon.

Spread a third of the batter, (about 2 cups) in pan. Sprinkle with a third of the filling, (about 6 tablespoons). Repeat twice, ending with filling on top. Bake for 1 hour, or until done.

Jacquie Fauth, Regina

Nuts and Seeds Bread

1½ cups white flour	2 tablespoons wheat germ
½ cup whole wheat flour	2 tablespoons sesame seeds
1 teaspoon baking powder	2 tablespoons poppy seeds
½ teaspoon baking soda	1 egg, beaten
½ teaspoon salt	1 cup buttermilk
1 cup brown sugar	¼ cup vegetable oil
½ cup chopped nuts	

Combine all dry ingredients and mix thoroughly. Combine egg, milk and oil. Then add to dry ingredients. Stir until blended.

Turn into a greased 9 x 5 inch pan or two smaller pans. Bake at 350°F. for 1 hour.

Linda Kurtz, Regina

Norwegian Bread

3 cups raisins	1 teaspoon salt
¼ cup butter	1 teaspoon cinnamon
2 cups boiling water	1 teaspoon baking soda
2 eggs, beaten	1 tablespoon boiling water
2 cups sugar	4 cups white flour
2 teaspoons vanilla	1 cup walnuts

Place raisins and butter in a glass or metal bowl. Pour 2 cups boiling water over raisins and butter. Mix. Cool 15 minutes.

Beat 2 eggs in a large mixing bowl. Add sugar, vanilla, salt, cinnamon and soda dissolved in water. Add raisin mixture. Chop walnuts. Add flour and walnuts. Mix well. Grease and flour two 9 x 5 x 2½ inch loaf pans. Pour mixture into pans. Bake at 350°F. for 60 minutes.

Sandra Dowie, Regina

Bishop's Bread

1	cup milk	⅓	cup chocolate chips
1	tablespoon vinegar	1	cup raisins
1	cup flour	¾	cup chopped red cherries
⅓	cup sugar	¾	cup chopped walnuts
½	teaspoon salt	¼	cup oil
½	teaspoon soda	1	beaten egg
1	cup rolled oats	1	teaspoon vanilla

Combine milk and vinegar; set aside. Sift together flour, sugar, salt and soda. Add oats, chips, raisins, cherries and walnuts, stirring to coat evenly with dry ingredients. Add milk-vinegar mixture, oil, egg and vanilla. Stir only until dry ingredients are moistened. Put mixture into a well greased loaf pan and bake at 325°F. for 60 to 65 minutes. Cool in pan for about 10 minutes then turn out on a rack.

Beverly Creusot, Regina

Applesauce Bread

2	cups flour	1	cup walnuts, coarsely chopped
¾	cup sugar		
1	tablespoon baking powder	1	egg, well beaten
1	teaspoon salt	1	cup medium thick applesauce
½	teaspoon baking soda	¼	cup cooking oil
½	teaspoon nutmeg		

Mix sifted dry ingredients and nuts together. Combine egg, applesauce and cooking oil. Add to dry ingredients and stir until just blended.

Pour into 5 x 9 inch greased loaf pan. Bake in moderate oven, 350°F. for 50 minutes.

Lynn Smith, Regina

Cinnamon Loaf

½	cup shortening	2	cups flour
¾	cup sugar	1	teaspoon baking powder
1	teaspoon vanilla	1	teaspoon baking soda
3	eggs	1	cup sour cream
6	tablespoons margarine	2	teaspoons cinnamon
1	cup brown sugar	½	cup chopped nuts

Cream together shortening, sugar, and vanilla. Add eggs and beat well. Sift together flour, baking powder and baking soda. Add flour mixture alternately with sour cream, to shortening mixture. Spread half of this mixture in an 8 x 8 inch pan.

Cream together margarine, brown sugar, cinnamon and nuts. Dot batter in pan with half the nut mixture. Add remaining batter to pan and dot with the remaining nut mixture. Bake at 350°F. for 50 minutes.

Cheryl Howe, Regina
Julia Westerman, Fort Qu'Appelle
Colleen Kasper, Regina
Doris Bell, Regina
Linda Kurtz, Regina
Lynn Smith, Regina

Banana Bread

¾	cup vegetable shortening	1	cup very ripe, mashed bananas
½	cup brown sugar		
½	cup white sugar	1	cup whole wheat flour
2	eggs	¾	cup white flour
½	teaspoon vanilla or orange extract	4	teaspoons baking powder
			dash of salt

Cream shortening and sugars. Beat in eggs and extract. Add mashed bananas; sift in flours, baking powder and salt. Mix thoroughly. Bake in a greased 9½ x 5½ x 3 inch loaf pan at 350°F. for 55 minutes. *This recipe contains no milk products and is suitable for milk sensitive people.*

Judy Jones, Regina
Ruth Griffiths, Prince Albert

French Onion Bread

- 5½ to 6 cups unbleached flour (or white enriched)
- 4 tablespoons dry onion soup mix (½ envelope)
- 3 tablespoons sugar
- 2 teaspoons salt
- 2 packages active dry yeast
- 2 tablespoons shortening
- 2 cups warm water
- 1 egg white, slightly beaten
- 1 tablespoon water

In a large mixer bowl combine 2 cups flour, onion soup mix, sugar, salt and dry yeast. Add shortening and warm water. Blend at lowest speed of mixer until moistened and then beat 3 minutes at medium speed. By hand, stir in remaining flour. Knead 3 minutes. Place in a greased bowl, cover and let rise 1 to 1½ hours.

Punch down, divide into two portions. Roll out into rectangles and roll into loaves. Let rise in loaf pans until light and doubled, 1 to 2 hours. Brush with egg white and water (beaten together), slash gently ½ inch deep in 4 to 5 places. Bake at 375°F. 35 to 40 minutes.

Makes 2 large loaves, or 24 hamburger buns. *This makes a great hit served warm with a company meal.*

Joan Brash, Regina

Zucchini Bread

3	eggs	¼	teaspoon baking powder
¾	cup oil	2	teaspoons baking soda
1¼	cups sugar	3	teaspoons cinnamon
2	cups grated zucchini	1	teaspoon salt
2	teaspoons vanilla	1	cup chopped walnuts
2	cups flour	¼	cup raisins

In a large bowl mix eggs, oil, sugar, zucchini and vanilla.

In another bowl mix the dry ingredients; and add to the zucchini mixture. Add the walnuts and raisins and stir to blend.

Pour into two well greased loaf pans. Bake for one hour at 375°F. Let cool for ten minutes, then remove from pan. *This is a dessert or tea bread similar to banana bread.*

Barbara Dreher, Delisle
Doris Bell, Regina
Sandra Gilewicz, Regina
Marion Isaacson, Saskatoon

Trinidadian Pita

1¼	cups warm water	1½	cups all-purpose flour
1	tablespoon oil	1½	cups whole wheat flour
1	tablespoon sugar	1	teaspoon salt
1	teaspoon yeast		cornmeal

Into a two-cup measuring cup, put the 1¼ cups water. Add oil and sugar and stir. Sprinkle yeast over top, stir once and let stand 15 minutes.

Into a large bowl measure flours and salt. Add risen yeast liquid and mix well. This is a firm dough and must be kneaded for 5 minutes. Return the dough to an oiled bowl and let rise for 3 hours.

Turn dough out on floured board and knead 25 times. Shape into long smooth 18 inch roll. Cut into 16 even pieces, shape each into a ball then with a rolling pin roll out into a ¼ inch thick round about 4 inches in diameter. Place on to cornmeal sprinkled baking sheets. You do not have to let them rise long this time, just while you are heating the oven to 425°F. Bake about 8 to 10 minutes.

Marilyn Nelson, Griffin

Grain Bread

½	cup honey	2	tablespoons granular yeast (2 packages)
1	cup hot water		
3½	cups hot water	2½	teaspoons salt
¼	cup molasses	½	cup vegetable oil
¾	cup bran	⅓	cup sesame seeds
⅓	cup flax seed	¾	cup wheat germ
5	cups stirred flour	¾	cup cracked wheat
5	cups whole wheat flour		

Mix honey and hot water. Stir until lukewarm. Sprinkle yeast on top. Let stand 15 minutes.

Mix hot water, molasses, salt and oil. Cool for 15 minutes.

Mix bran, flax, flours, sesame seeds, wheat germ and cracked wheat. Take 4 cups of the mixture and add to liquid. Stir until too thick to stir. Then add rest by kneading on a board. (about ½ hour). Leave ½ cup flour for shaping loaves. Put dough in bowl, oil top. Let rise until double in size. Knead. Cut into 3 equal pieces. Put flour on outside to shape loaves. Grease 3 bread pans. Let rise until 1 inch above top of pan. Put into cold oven. Turn heat to 350°F. Bake 35 to 40 minutes. *HINT: to make loaves rise faster place under a 40 or 60 watt light bulb for warmth.*

Louise Tunison, Regina

Cherry Loaf

1 cup white sugar
1 egg
⅛ teaspoon salt
½ cup butter
1 6 ounce bottle of red cherries, drained
Cherry juice plus milk, to make 1 cup
2 cups flour
2 teaspoons baking powder
½ cup raisins or walnuts (optional)

Cream together the sugar, egg, salt and butter. Add the cherries, using an electric mixer, and they will be cut into small pieces. Add the cherry juice and milk, flour and baking powder in order. Add raisins or walnuts if desired.

Pour into greased loaf pan, 9½ x 5½ x 3 inches, and bake for 70 minutes at 350°F., or until done.

Sandra Gilewicz, Regina

Date & Nut Loaf

1 cup chopped dates
1 teaspoon baking soda
1 cup boiling water
1 cup white sugar
2 tablespoons melted butter
1 egg
1½ cups flour
½ cup walnuts
1 teaspoon vanilla

Sprinkle the baking soda over the dates. Pour the boiling water over the dates and let it cool.

Mix together the sugar, melted butter and egg. Add the flour, walnuts and vanilla. Add the cooled date mixture and mix well.

Bake in a greased 8½ x 4½ x 2½ inch loaf pan at 350°F. for 50 to 60 minutes.

Janet West, Regina
Carol Martin, Ituna
Eileen Woodham, Regina

Swiss Christmas Bread

- ½ cup light cream
- ½ cup sugar
- 1 teaspoon salt
- ½ cup butter
- ½ cup lukewarm water
- 1 teaspoon sugar
- 2 tablespoons yeast
- 3 to 3½ cups flour
- 1 egg, beaten
- ¼ cup seedless raisins
- ¼ cup mixed candied fruit
- ¼ cup chopped nuts
- 1 tablespoon brandy extract
- ½ teaspoon cinnamon
- ½ teaspoon grated lemon peel

Scald cream in saucepan. Stir in sugar, salt and butter. Cool to lukewarm. Meanwhile dissolve yeast in water and sugar. Let stand 10 minutes. Stir in cream mixture and 1 cup flour, beat until smooth. Stir in beaten egg and add more flour to make a stiff dough. Knead until smooth. Place in greased bowl. Cover, let rise until doubled in bulk, about 45 minutes.

Meanwhile mix fruits, nuts, extract and cinnamon. Punch down dough; knead in fruit mixture. Cut dough into three equal parts. Shape each into a 14 inch roll and form into braid. Let rise until double (about 1 hour). Bake in moderate oven 325 to 350°F. for 40 to 45 minutes. Cool and frost with icing.

Icing:

- 2 cups sifted icing sugar
- 1 tablespoon lemon juice
- 2 tablespoons milk

Mix sugar, juice and milk. Spread on bread. *Decorate with cherries and almonds, if desired.*

Joyce Sloan, Regina

Hot Cross Buns

This traditional English recipe is made at Easter time and served Easter morning.

1½	cups milk	2	eggs, beaten
½	cup plus 1 tablespoon brown sugar	4	to 5½ cups flour
		2	teaspoons cinnamon
½	cup butter	1	teaspoon nutmeg
1	teaspoon salt	½	teaspoon ground cloves
2	packages active dry yeast	½	cup currents
		1	egg
¼	cup warm water	1	tablespoon milk
1	tablespoon sugar		

Scald 1½ cups milk; stir in the ½ cup brown sugar, butter and salt. Cool to lukewarm.

Sprinkle the yeast onto warm water in a large warm bowl. Stir until dissolved. Add 1 tablespoon each of brown and white sugars. Let stand for 10 minutes. Add lukewarm milk mixture and the two beaten eggs.

Sift 3 cups flour with the cinnamon, nutmeg and cloves. Add to mixing bowl and beat until smooth, about 4 minutes. Toss the currents with ½ cup flour and stir into the dough. Add enough additional flour to make a stiff dough. Turn out onto a lightly floured board; knead until smooth and elastic. Place in a large greased bowl, turning to grease top. Cover; let rise in a warm place, free from drafts, until doubled in size, about 1 hour.

Punch dough down and turn out onto a lightly floured board. Divide dough in half; cut each half into 12 equal pieces. Form each piece into a smooth round ball. Place on a greased cookie sheet about 2 inches apart. Cover; let rise in a warm place until doubled in size.

Preheat the oven to 400°F. Brush the tops of the buns with the 1 egg beaten with the 1 tablespoon of milk.

Bake about 20 minutes or until done. After 10 minutes of baking cover the buns with aluminum foil if they are browning too quickly.

Decorate each bun with a cross of sugar frosting.

Makes 24 buns.

Sugar Frosting:

1	cup icing sugar	½	teaspoon vanilla
2	tablespoons butter	1	to 2 tablespoons milk

Combine the sugar, butter, vanilla and add the milk until frosting reaches the desired spreading consistency.

Lois Olson, Regina

Homemade Bread

2	tablespoons yeast	3	tablespoons salt
1	cup warm water	½	cup lard
14	to 16 cups flour	6	cups warm water

Soak yeast in 1 cup warm water for 10 to 15 minutes. Place 5 cups flour in a large bowl. Add salt, lard dissolved in 6 cups water, and yeast mixture. Mix by hand until quite smooth. Keep adding flour (8 to 9 cups) until dough is no longer sticky. Knead another 5 minutes. Place well wrapped dough in a warm location for 2 hours. Knead dough and let rise for another 2 hours. Knead dough again and cut, shape, and put in pans. Let rise a further 3 hours. Bake at 375°F. for 45 minutes.

Yields 6 loaves.

Brenda Martin, Lumsden

Overnight Buns

3½ cups hot water
3 teaspoons salt
1 cup oil
1 cup sugar
2 eggs, well beaten
1 tablespoon vinegar
1 package yeast
1 teaspoon sugar
½ cup warm water
12 cups flour

At 5 p.m., mix together hot water, salt, oil, sugar, eggs and vinegar. Cool.

Sprinkle yeast over sugar dissolved in warm water, stir and let stand for 10 minutes.

Add yeast mixture to water mixture and stir. Add 12 cups of flour gradually, until stiff dough forms.

Knead well for 10 minutes. Let rise at room temperature and punch down at 8 p.m. Then at 9:30 p.m. shape into buns, cover with towels and leave overnight. At 8 or 9 a.m., bake at 375°F. for 15 minutes.

Makes about 8 dozen.

Sheena Wirges, Coderre
Carol Peterson, Regina

Quick Buns

1 tablespoon yeast
1 teaspoon sugar

1 cup boiling water
1 cup cold water
½ cup sugar

3 eggs

½ cup lukewarm water

3 tablespoons oil
1½ teaspoons salt

4 to 5 cups flour

Dissolve yeast and sugar in the lukewarm water, and let rise for 10 minutes.

Mix the boiling water and cold water, and pour it over the ½ cup sugar, oil and salt. Let stand while yeast is setting.

Beat the eggs, and add to the water mixture. Add the yeast. Add 3 cups of flour and beat well. Add more flour (to make a total of 4 to 5 cups) to make a stiff dough. Punch down every 15 minutes for first hour.

Shape into buns, then put in pan and let rise for 1 hour more.

Bake at 450°F. for 15 to 20 minutes.

Makes 2 to 3 dozen buns.

Gloria Libke, Regina

Air Buns

½	cup lukewarm water	2	teaspoons salt
1	teaspoon white sugar	2	tablespoons vinegar
1	package yeast	3½	cups lukewarm water
½	cup white sugar	8	to 10 cups flour
½	cup lard		

Mix ½ cup water and 1 teaspoon sugar and yeast in a bowl, and let stand for 10 minutes.

In a large bowl put ½ cup sugar, lard, salt, vinegar and 3½ cups lukewarm water. Add yeast mixture and 8 to 10 cups of flour, with mixing, to form a stiff dough. Put in a greased bowl and let rise 2 hours.

Knead, let rise 1 more hour. Knead again, and form buns. Place them on greased cookie sheets, and let rise 3 hours. *NOTE: For spudnuts, add 1 cup mashed potatoes and 2 eggs. Rise as above. Cut into donuts and deep dry.*

Bake at 325°F. for 30 minutes.

Makes 5 to 6 dozen buns.

Loretta Ball, Regina
Olga Hill, Regina
Marlene Deshaies, Regina

Cinnamon Buns

- 1 cup warm water
- 2 teaspoons sugar
- 2 packages active dry yeast
- ½ cup milk
- ¼ cup margarine
- ½ cup sugar
- 1½ teaspoons salt
- 2 eggs (beaten)
- 4 to 5 cups all-purpose flour
- 1½ cups brown sugar
- ⅔ cup seedless raisins
- 2 teaspoons ground cinnamon

Measure 1 cup warm water into large bowl. Stir in 2 teaspoons sugar and the yeast. Let stand 10 minutes then stir well.

Combine milk and margarine in a saucepan. Heat over low heat until liquid is warm and margarine melts. Stir in ½ cup sugar and the salt. Add liquid to the dissolved yeast. Add eggs and 1½ cups flour. Stir in additional 3 cups flour to make soft dough. Turn out onto lightly floured board; knead until smooth and elastic, about 8 to 10 minutes. Place in a greased bowl, turning to grease the top. Cover and let rise in a warm place, free from draft, until doubled in bulk, about 1 hour.

Punch dough down; turn out onto lightly floured board. Divide in half. Roll each half into an 18 x 9 inch oblong. Brush with melted margarine. Combine 1½ cups sugar, ⅔ cup raisins and cinnamon. Sprinkle half of the mixture over each piece of dough. Roll each up as for jelly roll, to make 18 inch rolls. Seal edges firmly. Cut each roll into 12 pieces, about 1½ inches wide. Place cut side up, in 2 greased 9 inch round cake pans, or 2 greased 8 inch square pans. Cover and let rise in warm place, free from draft, until doubled in bulk, about 1 hour.

Bake at 350°F. about 25 minutes, or until done. Remove from pans and cool on wire racks. Serve plain or frosted.

Makes 2 dozen cinnamon buns.

Lynn Harrison, Semans

Cheddar Bread

- 2 cups all-purpose flour
- 4 teaspoons baking powder
- 1 teaspoon white sugar
- ½ teaspoon onion salt
- ¼ teaspoon oregano
- ¼ teaspoon garlic powder
- ¼ teaspoon dry mustard
- 1¼ cups shredded Cheddar cheese (10 ounces)
- 1 egg, well beaten
- 1 cup milk
- 1 tablespoon melted butter

Stir together in a bowl the flour, baking powder, sugar, seasonings and cheese.

Combine egg, milk and butter; add all at once to dry ingredients, stirring until just moistened.

Spread batter in a greased 9½ x 5½ x 3 inch loaf pan. Bake in preheated oven at 350°F. for 45 minutes, remove from pan, slice and serve. *This recipe is especially good with Italian food.*

Carol Biggin, Regina
Dianne McEwan, Regina

Corn Bread

- 1 cup flour
- 1 teaspoon salt
- 3 teaspoons baking powder
- 1 cup cornmeal
- ½ cup brown sugar
- ¾ cup milk
- 3 tablespoons corn syrup
- 1 egg, well beaten
- 2 tablespoons cooking oil

Combine flour, salt, baking powder, cornmeal and brown sugar in a mixing bowl. Combine milk, syrup and egg and turn this mixture into blended dry ingredients. Add cooking oil. Stir just to blend. Pour batter into greased 8 x 8 inch pan. Bake for 20 minutes at 425°F.

Karen Haggman, Regina

Nachinka
Corn Meal Dressing

1	small onion	1	teaspoon salt
3	to 4 slices bacon (cut up)	1	quart warm milk
¼	pound butter	4	well-beaten eggs
1	cup cornmeal	1	teaspoon baking powder
¼	cup sugar		

Fry the chopped onion and bacon in butter until golden brown. Turn the heat to low. Add cornmeal and mix well. Add sugar, salt and warm milk. Stir slowly until cornmeal begins to thicken. Remove from heat. Add the well-beaten eggs and baking powder. Mix well together and place in a 325°F. oven for 1 hour.

Rose Carsten, Regina
Faithe Prodanuk, Saskatoon

Katorshnik
(Russian Potato Cake)

2	cups riced potatoes	½	cup fresh cream
4	eggs, separated	1	heaping teaspoon baking powder
½	teaspoon salt		

Cook potatoes in boiling salted water until tender. Drain and put through a potato ricer. Set aside.

Beat egg yolks; add salt and cream, then add riced potatoes. Fold in stiffly beaten egg whites and baking powder and mix gently, but well. Put into a well greased 8 x 10 inch pan and bake in a 400°F. oven for 20 to 25 minutes or until done and nicely browned. *Serve hot with melted butter.*

Myra Siminoff, Melville

Yorkshire Pudding

2	eggs	¼	teaspoon salt
1	cup milk	1	teaspoon baking powder
1	cup flour		

Beat eggs until light. Add remaining ingredients and beat well. Cover bottom of 8 x 8 inch pan with drippings from roast. Pour in batter.

Bake at 425°F. for 20 minutes. Cut in squares and serve hot with roast beef.

For individual puddings, bake 15 minutes in greased preheated muffin tins.

Kae Cheney, Saskatoon
Lynn Smith, Regina
Doris Bell, Regina
Sharon Holliday, Regina
Kathy Seidlitz, Richardson

Apple Pancakes

1¼	cups all-purpose flour	1	cup milk
2½	teaspoons baking powder	3	tablespoons melted butter or oil
3	tablespoons sugar		
½	teaspoon salt	1	cup pared and shredded dessert apples
¼	teaspoon cinnamon		
2	eggs (separated, whites stiffly beaten)		

Sift together the flour, baking powder, sugar, salt and cinnamon. Stir in the egg yolks, milk and melted butter or oil. Shred the apple and immediately add it to the batter. Fold in stiffly beaten egg whites. Drop by tablespoonful and fry on greased griddle until bubbly. Turn over and brown on other side. *Use more milk for thin large pancakes. The best yet!*

Joyce Tourney, Regina

Lyszniki

2 eggs, well beaten
1½ cups milk
1 tablespoon sugar
¼ teaspoon vanilla

1¼ cups flour
1½ teaspoons baking powder
¼ teaspoon salt

Cheese Filling:

2 cups creamed cottage cheese
2 eggs, well beaten
¼ teaspoon salt

1 tablespoon sugar
1 tablespoon chopped dill
sweet cream to pour over pancakes

To make the batter, mix eggs, milk, and 1 tablespoon sugar together. Add vanilla. Sift flour, baking powder and salt together and add to milk mixture, stirring until smooth. Using a greased frying pan, fry the batter into thin pancakes.

To make the filling, mix cottage cheese, eggs, salt, 1 tablespoon sugar and dill. Spread each pancake with filling and roll up like a jelly roll. Arrange in a well buttered casserole, and pour sweet cream over all.

Bake at 275°F. for 35 minutes. Uncover towards the end so that they will brown a little.

Pat Mialkowsky, Saskatoon

Bannock

2 cups flour
2 teaspoons baking powder
1 teaspoon salt

⅓ cup oil
⅔ cup milk

Mix ingredients together with a fork. Knead lightly. Place in a greased 9 inch pie plate. Bake at 425°F. till lightly browned. *Delicious with jam and butter.*

Variations:

add: ½ cup grated cheese or 1 teaspoon garlic powder, basil or oregano

Joanne Sorenson, Glaslyn

Scuffles

1	package yeast	½	cup milk
¼	cup lukewarm water	2	eggs, well-beaten
3	cups flour	1	cup white sugar
½	teaspoon salt	2	tablespoons cinnamon
3	tablespoons sugar		
1	cup soft butter or margarine		

Dissolve yeast in warm water and let stand 10 minutes.

Mix the flour, salt, 3 tablespoons sugar and butter or margarine as for pie crust.

Add to the dry ingredients and milk and eggs, and the yeast mixture. Mix well and knead dough until soft. Put in a bowl, cover and store in the refrigerator overnight. This dough is very soft and must be chilled before use.

Divide dough into 6 parts, keeping one part out and putting the rest back in the fridge until ready for it. Roll dough out on a mixture of the 1 cup sugar and cinnamon. Try to keep the shape of the rolled dough as round as possible. Cut into wedges, 12 per round if the thickness is ⅛ inch. Roll from wide end to narrow end. Place on a lightly greased baking sheet about 1 inch apart and bake for 15 to 20 minutes at 350°F. Remove from baking sheet immediately and cool well. These freeze very well. *If you wish to prepare a few pans before baking keep them in the fridge until ready for baking, otherwise they will start to rise.*

Pat Mialkowsky, Saskatoon
Brenda Martin, Lumsden
Pat Bergquist, Guernsey
Sharon Holliday, Regina

Waffles

2	cups flour	1¼	cups milk
2	teaspoons baking powder	⅓	cup shortening
½	teaspoon salt	2	teaspoons sugar
3	eggs, separated		

Sift flour with dry ingredients. Beat egg yolks in separate bowl and add milk, shortening, then stir into flour immediately. Beat until smooth.

Beat egg whites until stiff, then add sugar. Beat until stiff. Fold egg whites into batter. Bake in hot waffle iron using ½ cup batter for each waffle.

Judy McDonald, Assiniboia

Potato Pancakes

1	cup pared, diced, raw potatoes	½	teaspoon salt
		1	tablespoon oil
2	eggs	¼	cup milk
⅓	cup flour	½	small onion (optional)

Keep potatoes in cold water. Put eggs in blender container and blend until frothy. Add flour, salt, oil, milk, and onion. Dry potato chunks and add. Grind or blend until smooth. Pour onto skillet and cook until brown.

Serve with applesauce, syrup, sour cream, sausages or bacon.

Makes 12 pancakes (3 inches in diameter).

Gertrude Beck, Swift Current
Adeline Wilson, Archerwill

Crepes Suzette

- ⅔ cup sifted all-purpose flour
- 2 tablespoons sugar
- 1½ cups milk
- 2 eggs
- 2 egg yolks
- 2 tablespoons butter or margarine, melted
- ⅛ teaspoon salt

Filling:

- ½ cup butter or margarine
- ½ cup sugar
- 2 teaspoons grated orange peel
- 1 teaspoon grated lemon peel
- ¼ cup orange juice
- 1 tablespoon lemon juice
- confectioner's sugar
- ¼ cup orange flavored liqueur

To make the crepes, combine flour, 2 tablespoons sugar, milk, eggs, egg yolks, 2 tablespoons butter and salt. Beat until smooth. Lightly grease a 6 inch skillet and heat. Remove from heat, and spoon in about 2 tablespoons of batter. Rotate pan so batter is spread evenly over bottom. Return to heat and brown on one side only. To remove, invert pan over paper toweling. Repeat with remaining batter, greasing pan occasionally. Keep warm until served.

To make the filling, cream the ½ cup butter and ½ cup sugar; add grated peels and fruit juices. Spread about 1 tablespoon of filling on each crepe. Roll up and sprinkle with confectioner's sugar. *At serving time, arrange filled crepes in a chafing dish. Place over burner. In small saucepan, heat liqueur, ignite and spoon over crepes.*

Makes 6 servings.

Joan Isaak, Regina

Hush Puppies (Corn Fritters)

1½	cups yellow cornmeal	1	egg, beaten
½	cup flour	¾	cup milk
2	teaspoons baking powder	1	tablespoon minced onion
½	teaspoon salt		(optional)
⅛	teaspoon pepper		vegetable oil (for deep frying)

Sift together dry ingredients. Beat egg until light and fluffy. Stir in milk and onion. Add gradually to dry ingredients and mix.

Heat oil to 375°F. Drop batter into oil by heaping teaspoonsful. Fry until golden brown, turning as they brown. Drain on paper towels.

Good with soup or salad.

Makes 2 dozen.

Norma Vik, Saskatoon

Baking Powder Biscuits

2	cups flour	½	teaspoon cream of tartar
4	teaspoons baking powder	½	cup shortening
½	teaspoon salt	⅔	cup milk
2	tablespoons sugar	1	egg, unbeaten

Sift dry ingredients into a bowl. Blend in shortening until mixture resembles cornmeal. Pour milk in slowly; add egg. Stir until it is a stiff dough. Turn out onto a floured board. Lightly knead 5 times. Roll out to ¾ to 1 inch thickness. Cut with a 1½ inch cutter. Bake 10 to 15 minutes at 450°F.

Makes 1½ to 2 dozen biscuits.

Sharon Luft, Tisdale
Jacquie Fauth, Regina
Christina Patoine, Regina

Scottish Tea Scones

2½ cups flour
¾ teaspoon sugar
½ teaspoon salt
½ teaspoon baking soda
½ teaspoon baking powder
⅓ teaspoon cream of tartar
¾ to 1 cup buttermilk

Mix the dry ingredients together. Add enough buttermilk to produce a firm dough. Knead dough lightly and form into a 10 x 10 x ½ inch square. Cut into 4 wedges and bake in a hot dry electric frying pan, 450°F., until bottom is lightly browned. Flip and cook the top side the same way. *These scones are delicious served warm with butter, jam or cheese for a tea treat. When scones are cooled, you may split them in half and fry in hot bacon fat, then serve for breakfast with a fried egg on top, accompanied by bacon.*

Pat Anderson, Regina

Welsh Tea Cakes

5 cups flour
1½ cups white sugar
2 tablespoons baking powder
1 pound margarine
1 cup currants or raisins
2 beaten eggs
½ cup milk

Mix dry ingredients, cut in margarine. Add currants or raisins.

Beat eggs and milk together and pour into dry ingredients. Mix well.

Roll dough out ¼ inch thick and cut into squares or rounds. Cook in electric fry pan or griddle at 325°F. for 6 to 7 minutes per side.

Makes 5 or 6 dozen.

Donna Flotre, Regina

Orange Butter Crescents

Dough:

1	package yeast	1	teaspoon salt
¼	cup warm water	2	eggs
1	teaspoon sugar	¼	cup sugar
6	tablespoons margarine	2¾	to 3¼ cups flour
½	cup sour cream		

Filling:

¾	cup sugar	2	tablespoons orange rind
¾	cup coconut		

Glaze:

¾	cup sugar	2	tablespoons orange juice
½	cup sour cream	¼	cup melted butter

Dissolve yeast in warm water and sugar, stir and let stand for 10 minutes.

Melt the margarine, and add sour cream, salt, eggs and sugar. Blend well, then add yeast and gradually add the flour to make a stiff dough. Knead slightly. Cover and let rise 2 hours.

Combine sugar, coconut, and orange rind. Divide dough in half. Roll each half into a 12 inch circle. Brush with butter and sprinkle with half coconut mixture on each. Cut circle into 12 wedges and roll up, wide end to point. Place seam side down in a 13 x 9 inch greased baking dish. Put fairly close together. Bake at 350°F. for 30 minutes or until done.

Mix sugar, sour cream, orange juice and melted butter to make glaze. Pour over hot rolls.

Jacquie Fauth, Regina

Preserving A Husband

Be careful in your selection. Do not choose too young or too old. When once selected, give your entire thoughts to preparation for domestic use.

Some insist upon keeping them in hot water. This may make them sour, hard and sometimes bitter.

Even poor varieties may be made sweet and tender and good by garnishing them with patience, well sweetened with love and seasoned with kisses.

Wrap them in kindness and consideration. Keep warm with a steady fire of domestic devotion and serve with peaches and cream.

Thus prepared, they will keep for years!

Canning & Condiments

**SAUCES
JAMS
RELISHES
PICKLES**

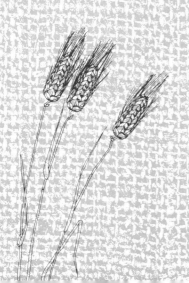
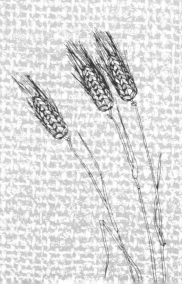

Pizza Bun Mix

1 pound Velveeta cheese	1 teaspoon oregano
½ pound mozzarella cheese	¼ to ½ teaspoon cayenne pepper
1 pound bacon, cut into small pieces	salt and pepper to taste
1 medium onion, chopped	
1 10 ounce can tomato soup	

Melt Velveeta and mozzarella cheese in a double boiler.

In a fry pan, cook bacon and onion. Drain off the fat.

Mix together the soup, oregano, cayenne pepper and salt and pepper. Add the bacon-onion mixture and mix with the melted cheese.

Put on buns, English muffins, or French bread and boil approximately 5 minutes. Green peppers and mushrooms may be added prior to broiling, if desired. *NOTE: Store this pizza mix in a sealer in the refrigerator. Keeps about 3 months. NOTE: This recipe can also be prepared in a microwave oven.*

Julia Westerman, Fort Qu'Appelle

Tartar Sauce

1 cup mayonnaise	1 tablespoon chopped green olives
1 teaspoon prepared mustard	1 finely chopped hard boiled egg
1 tablespoon finely chopped parsley	1 tablespoon chopped capers
1 tablespoon chopped sweet pickle	

Mix all ingredients. *Especially tasty as a sauce for fish.*

Joanne Sorenson, Glaslyn

Chili Sauce

20	ripe tomatoes	½	teaspoon cloves
8	large onions, chopped	¼	teaspoon pepper
10	apples, cooked	½	teaspoon salt
2½	cups vinegar	¼	teaspoon cayenne
2½	cups white sugar	1	red pepper cut into pieces
1	cup celery, chopped		
1	teaspoon dry mustard	2	teaspoons pickling spice
1	heaping teaspoon cinnamon		

Pour boiling water over the tomatoes and then cover with cold water. Skin. Add the remaining ingredients to the tomatoes in a large dutch oven. Put the mixed pickling spices in a cheesecloth bag and place it in with the tomato mixture. Boil for about 1½ hours. Remove the spice bag and pour into sterilized sealers and seal.

Gayle Thompson, Semans

Beer Batter For Fondue

¾	cup flour	½	teaspoon nutmeg
¼	cup corn starch	2	eggs, slightly beaten
1	teaspoon baking powder	½	cup beer (may be flat)
2	teaspoons salt		

Mix together flour, corn starch, baking powder, salt and nutmeg. Add eggs and beer. Beat until creamy and smooth. *Use to coat pieces of vegetables, fruit, meat, etc. before dropping into hot vegetable oil in your fondue pot.*

Ruth Griffiths, Prince Albert

Tomato Ketchup

36	ripe tomatoes	2	sticks cinnamon
1	cup chopped onion	½	teaspoon whole cloves
¾	cup chopped red sweet pepper	2	teaspoons whole allspice
3	tablespoons salt	1½	teaspoons mustard seed
½	cup white sugar	1	teaspoon celery seed
1½	cups vinegar	½	teaspoon chili corn

Clean and chop the tomatoes. Place the vegetables, salt, sugar, vinegar and cinnamon sticks in a large stainless steel pot.

Make a spice bag from a gauze containing all the other spices. Add the spice bag to the tomato mixture and cook 20 minutes. Press through a sieve. Reduce liquid by simmering, until it has the texture of ketchup. Pour into sterilized containers.

Pat Anderson, Regina

Chocolate Fudge Sauce

4	tablespoons butter	2	cups sugar
4	squares unsweetened chocolate	¼	cup corn syrup
⅔	cup boiling water	¼	teaspoon salt
		2	teaspoons vanilla

Melt butter in 3 quart saucepan over low heat. Add chocolate and melt. Stir in hot water, sugar, corn syrup and salt. Bring to a boil over medium heat. Cook without stirring until sauce is thickened, dark and glossy, about 6 to 8 minutes. Stir in vanilla. *Refrigerate leftover. Reheat before using.*

Makes about 2 cups.

Jacquie Fauth, Regina

Butterscotch Cream Sauce

- 1 cup brown sugar
- ¼ cup flour
- ¼ teaspoon salt
- 1¼ cups cold water
- ¼ pound margarine
- 1 teaspoon vanilla extract
- ½ pint whipping cream

Mix the brown sugar, flour and salt together. Then add water, and mix well in a saucepan. Boil until thick, stirring constantly. When there is no more taste of flour (about 5 minutes) remove from the heat. Add the margarine and vanilla, and mix. Pour into a large mixing bowl and refrigerate.

When the sauce is cold, whip it up thoroughly. Whip the whipping cream until stiff peaks form and then stir into the butterscotch mixture. Keep cool. *This sauce is especially delicious served over spice cake or any of your favorite white cakes. If refrigerated for more than a day, the syrup may separate from the sauce, but gentle stirring will restore it again.*

The recipe makes enough sauce to serve generously with an 8 x 8 inch cake.

Christina Patoine, Regina

Rhubarb Jam

- 5 cups fresh rhubarb, chopped
- 5 cups white sugar
- 1 20 ounce can crushed pineapple, undrained
- 1 6 ounce package strawberry jello powder

In a saucepan combine rhubarb, sugar and canned pineapple and boil gently for 20 minutes. Then stir in the strawberry jello powder until dissolved. Pour into sterilized jam jars and seal with double coating of new melted parafin. *Frozen rhubarb may also be used if desired, in which case, you should drain the pineapple to reduce the liquid. Otherwise, the jam will be too thin.*

Doris Bell, Regina

Zucchini and Apple Chutney

6	cups grated zucchini	½	teaspoon cloves
3	cups finely chopped apples (or crabapples)	½	teaspooon nutmeg
		½	teaspoon ginger
1	cup chopped onion	¼	teaspoon allspice
1	clove garlic, finely chopped	⅛	teaspoon cayenne pepper
1	4½ ounce can sweet red peppers, cut up	3	cups sugar, white and/or brown
		2	cups vinegar
1	cup raisins	½	cup chopped nuts
½	teaspoon cinnamon		

Mix all ingredients in a large kettle and bring to a boil. Reduce heat and simmer until clear and thickened, stirring occasionally. Near end of cooking add the ½ cup of chopped nuts (more may be used if desired). Pack in sterile jars, and seal. Label and store in cool dry place.

Muriel Barsaloux, Saskatoon

Heavenly Jam

2	lemons	12	pears
4	oranges	12	apples
12	peaches		white sugar

Wash oranges and lemons. Put through food chopper. Cover with water and let stand overnight.

In the morning place the fruit and water over low heat and boil gently until tender. Pare and cut the peaches, pears and apples. Mix with the cooked ingredients. Measure fruit and add one cup sugar for each cup of fruit. Boil rapidly, uncovered. Stir often until thick and clear.

Seal in sterilized jars.

Doris Bell, Regina

Beet Jelly

2	or 3 large beets	1	box certo
5	cups water	4	cups white sugar
1	package grape freshie or lemon freshie		

Peel and slice beets into small pieces and boil in water until beets lose their color. Measure 3 cups of this beet juice and add the package of freshie. Then add certo and bring to a boil. Add sugar and bring mixture back to a boil for 6 minutes. Pour into sealers and seal while hot. *If lemon freshie is used, jelly tastes like pincherries.*

Marlene Deshaies, Regina
Evelyn Hull, Willowbrook

Pancake Syrup

½ cup honey   ½ cup butter

Place ingredients in a saucepan. Melt over low heat. Pour over pancakes.

Variations:

add grated orange peel
add fresh grated nutmeg
add ½ cup diced fresh fruit

Joanne Sorenson, Glaslyn

Beet — Horseradish Relish

4	cups finely chopped cooked beets	1	cup grated horseradish
		1	tablespoon pickling salt
4	cups finely chopped raw cabbage	2	cups vinegar
		2	cups white sugar

Combine beets, cabbage and horseradish and mix thoroughly. Sprinkle salt over mixed vegetables. Mix well. Scald the vinegar, dissolve the sugar in it. Add combined vegetables with the salt (don't drain!). Heat together and cook until vegetables are clear. Pack into hot sterilized jars and seal while hot. *The beets and cabbage may be finely chopped with a knife or put through a food chopper. If the latter method is used, the relish will not be crisp. After long storage, beet relish sometimes has a tendency to fade. For this reason it should be used up more quickly than other pickles and relishes that are more "color stable". Storing in a cool, very dark place prolongs shelf life.*

Yields 4 pint sealers.

Pearl Fahlman, Fillmore

Fresh Onion Cucumber Relish

2	medium sweet onions, chopped	3	tablespoons cider vinegar (or white)
1	peeled cucumber, sliced thinly	1	teaspoon salt
		¼	cup minced parsley

Place all ingredients in screwtop jar. Cover, give a few shakes and let stand covered for 2 days to 3 weeks. Shake well before serving. *This relish loses its crispness if not kept cool, but does not spoil or lose its flavor.*

Jacquie Fauth, Regina

Beet Relish

- 10 beets, cooked and diced in ½ inch cubes
- 2 heads celery, chopped medium fine
- 3 large onions, chopped
- 2 tablespoons dry mustard
- 3 tablespoons flour
- ¼ cup cold vinegar
- 1½ cups hot vinegar
- 2 cups brown sugar
- salt to taste

Place beets, celery and onions in a large cooking pot. Prepare sauce by mixing mustard and flour with ¼ cup cold vinegar. Add 1½ cups heated vinegar and the brown sugar. Cook for 5 minutes until slightly thick and partially clear. Add salt.

Pour sauce over the vegetables and heat through until steamy. Bottle in sterile jars. *Use as side salad or relish tray.*

Makes 4 quarts.

Peggi Talbot, Regina

Vegetable Relish Maranata

- 1 cauliflower, broken into flowerets
- 3 carrots, cut into 3 inch strips
- 2 ribs of celery, cut into 1 inch pieces
- 1 green pepper, cut in strips
- 1 4 ounce jar pimento (optional)
- ½ cup green olives
- 1 cup green beans, cut in 3 inch pieces
- ¾ cup vinegar
- ¾ cup water
- ½ cup oil
- 2 tablespoons sugar
- 1 teaspoon salt
- ¼ teaspoon pepper
- ¾ teaspoon oregano

Combine all ingredients in a large saucepan and bring to a boil. Simmer covered for 8 to 10 minutes. Refrigerate 24 hours before serving.

Norma Vik, Saskatoon

Antipasto

1	small cauliflower	1	pound jar dill pickles
1	pound tiny pickling onions (or a 12 ounce jar sweet pickling onions)	1	14 ounce can black olives
		4	7 ounce cans tuna
		4	4½ ounce cans small shrimp (or anchovies)
3	green peppers		
3	red peppers	½	cup vinegar
1	14 ounce can green beans	½	cup vegetable oil
4	10 ounce cans mushrooms	1	40 ounce bottle ketchup

Cut cauliflower and onions into small pieces and cook until tender crisp. Cut remaining vegetables, pickles and olives into small pieces.

Flake tuna, and chop shrimp or anchovies into a separate bowl.

Combine all ingredients in a large pot and cook together for 15 minutes over low heat. Pour into sterilized jars and seal. Process for 30 minutes in a boiling water bath or keep frozen. *Use as a relish, or on crackers as a garnish.*

Bertha Eyre, Saskatoon
Anita Veikle, Cut Knife

Pickled Eggs

3	cups white vinegar	1	bay leaf
2	teaspoons white sugar	½	piece chili pepper (can be taken from a pickling spice package)
1	teaspoon salt		
½	teaspoon mustard seed		
4	whole cloves		about 18 hard boiled eggs

Put vinegar, sugar, salt and spices into a large saucepan and bring to a boil. Fill a 2 quart sealer with the eggs and strain the hot liquid over them. Seal the jar and invert to cool. Leave for 5 days.

Kathy Keller, Regina

Green Tomato Mincemeat

6	cups chopped green tomatoes	4	cups brown sugar
6	cups chopped apples	1	cup mixed peel
3	cups raisins (or 2 cups raisins and 1 cup currants)	1	teaspoon cinnamon
		1	teaspoon cloves
		¾	teaspoon allspice
		¾	teaspoon mace
1	cup butter or margarine	2	teaspoons salt
¾	cup vinegar		

Pour cold water over tomatoes, bring to a boil and drain. Do this 2 more times. Add remaining ingredients and bring to a boil, simmer till clear and thick, about 1½ hours. Seal in jars.

Makes 8 pints.

Irene Nagel, Moose Jaw
Sandra Gilewicz, Regina

Pickled Beets

1 cup white sugar
1 cup brown sugar
1 teaspoon pickling salt
2 cups vinegar
2 cups water
2 teaspoons pickling spices tied in a cheesecloth bag
small beets to fill 4 to 5 quart sealers

To make brine, bring to a boil the sugars, pickling salt, vinegar, water and pickling spices.

Cook beets in their skins until tender. Drain, pour cold water over them. Peel. Cut into pieces, place in sterilized sealers. Pour brine over so that the beets are covered. Seal.

Loretta Ball, Regina
Maureen Materi, Lipton

Bread and Butter Pickles

20	medium sized cucumbers, unpeeled	5	cups white sugar
8	small onions, peeled	5	cups white vinegar
2	medium sized green peppers, cored	½	teaspoon turmeric
½	cup coarse salt	½	teaspoon cloves
4	to 5 dozen ice cubes	2	teaspoons mustard seed
		2	teaspoons celery seed

Wash and slice the cucumbers, onions and green peppers, crosswise. Layer them in a large flat-bottomed container (such as a dishpan or a roaster bottom). Sprinkle the vegetables with the coarse salt and cover them with ice cubes. Weigh everything down the best you can with plates or heavy pot lids, and leave sitting overnight. (Or a minimum of 4 hours).

Remove the plates or lids and rinse the vegetables well with cold water. Drain.

To make the brine, mix the vinegar, sugar and spices in a large dutch oven. Bring to a boil and boil 5 minutes. Add the vegetables, stir gently, and bring just to a boil again. Ladle vegetables and brine into sterile quart sealers, bringing liquid level to the top of the jar. Seal, stand the jars upside down until cooled to insure that they are sealed. *Can be sampled in about 4 weeks!*

Makes about 6 quarts of pickles.

Christina Patoine, Regina
Pat Anderson, Regina

Dilled Bean Pickles

approximately 1 quart yellow wax beans
¼ cup coarse salt
sprigs of dill
¼ cup vinegar
1 teaspoon coarse salt
2 cups water

Cut ends off of yellow beans and wash well. Put beans in a deep pot and add the ¼ cup salt and enough water to cover beans. Bring to a boil and simmer until beans are barely tender. Drain and pack hot beans in jars with fresh dill between.

To prepare brine, boil vinegar, 1 teaspoon salt and water together. Pour over beans while still hot to fill jars and seal.

Ruth Griffiths, Prince Albert

Dill Pickles

Cucumbers to fill a 2 quart sealer
1 tablespoon pickling salt
1 large chili pepper
2 to 3 toes of chopped garlic
1 horseradish leaf (this keeps the pickles firmer)
dill

Wash cucumbers and pack in the 2 quart sealer, with dill head on top and bottom of the sealer.

Add the spices and salt. Fill the jar with cold water and leave at room temperature 4 to 5 days. *This recipe is excellent for dilling carrots and beans as well.*

Boil carrots for 10 minutes, or beans for 5 minutes. Rinse them in cold water, then follow the recipe as for dilled cucumbers.

Maureen Materi, Lipton

Sweet Dill Pickles

½	cup coarse salt	1 teaspoon celery seed
16	cups water	3 cups sugar
12	large cucumbers	1 teaspoon turmeric
3	cups vinegar	dill seed
1	tablespoon coarse salt	alum

Mix together the ½ cup salt and water. Slice the cucumbers in slices about ¼ inches in width. Place them in the salt water and let stand for 2 hours, then drain.

In a large kettle boil together the vinegar, 1 tablespoon salt, sugar and spices to make the brine. Place the drained cucumbers in this brine and simmer for 5 minutes. Place in jars and add 1 teaspoon dill seed and a pinch of alum to the top of each jar. Seal the jars well.

Marlene Deshaies, Regina

Kitchen Tricks On Conversion

Imperial			Metric	

Liquid:

1	ounce	=	28	millilitres
1	cup (8 ounces)	=	225	millilitres
2½	cups (1 pint)	=	500	millilitres
2	pints (1 quart)	=	1.12	litres
4	quarts (1 gallon)	=	4.5	litres
0.88	quarts	=	1	litre

Dry:

1	teaspoon	=	5	millilitres
1	tablespoon	=	15	millilitres
¼	cup	=	60	millilitres
1	cup (16 tablespoons)	=	250	millilitres
2	cups	=	500	millilitres

Mass:

1	ounce	=	28	millilitres
4.4	ounces	=	125	millilitres
8.8	ounces	=	250	millilitres
17.6	ounces	=	500	millilitres
35.3	ounces	=	1000	millilitres
1	pound	=	0.45	litres
1000	pounds	=	454.4	litres
2205	pounds	=	1	tonne

Temperature:

Fahrenheit	Celsius
500°	260°
450°	230°
400°	200°
350°	180°
300°	150°
250°	120°
200°	95°
150°	65°

When baking in ovenproof glassware, reduce the temperature by 10°C. (or 25° F.).

Simple Substitutions

I thought I had . . .

Baking powder — to equal 1 teaspoon of baking powder, use ¼ teaspoon baking soda plus ½ teaspoon cream of tartar.

Buttermilk or Sour milk — 1 cup of milk plus 1 tablespoon vinegar or lemon juice. Let stand for 5 minutes.

Honey (1 cup) — 1¼ cups white sugar plus ¼ cup of any liquid.

Corn Syrup (½ cup) — ½ cup white sugar plus 2 tablespoons of any liquid.

Chocolate, unsweetened (1 ounce) — 3 tablespoons cocoa plus 1 tablespoon shortening.

Fresh herbs (1 teaspoon) — ⅓ to ½ teaspoon of dried herb.

Whole egg — use ½ teaspoon of baking powder for each egg required
    — or, increase the amount of liquid called for by ½ cup
    — or, use just 2 egg yolks.

Nuts — use oatmeal browned in small amount of butter.

Bread Crumbs — use corn flakes, wheat flakes, or any unsweetened cereal.

Sour Cream — 1 cup plain yogurt or evaporated milk plus 1 tablespoon vinegar
    — or, 1 cup cottage cheese blended with 2 tablespoons milk and 1 teaspoon lemon juice.

Whipped Cream — beat egg whites until stiff and add 1 sliced banana per egg white used and beat again until banana is dissolved
    — or, add melted marshmallows to the white of an egg and beat until stiff

Flour, for thickening (1 tablespoon) — use ½ tablespoon cornstarch
- or, 1 tablespoon minute tapioca
- or, ¼ to ½ cup soft bread crumbs
- or, 1 ounce chocolate
- or, 1 egg

Sugar (1 cup, granulated) — 1 cup packed brown sugar
- or, 1½ cups molasses plus ½ tablespoon baking soda (reduce liquid by ¼ cup)
- or, 1 cup corn syrup (reduce liquid by ¼ cup)
- or, 1 cup honey (reduce liquid by ¼ cup)

Household Hints

Add a few tablespoons of vinegar to dishwater to cut the grease.

To clean counter-tops scrub vigorously with a paste of baking soda and water. Let sit for ½ hour. Wipe with wet sponge.

Ovens

Put removable parts into a plastic garbage bag, and pour in a couple of cups of ammonia. Seal and leave several hours. Slit bottom over sink to drain. Open and rinse. In summer, this can be done outside with the garden hose.

If something spills or boils over in a hot oven, sprinkle with salt immediately. When cool, brush off burned food and wipe clean with a damp sponge.

Baking Hints

Butter new tins and place in moderate oven for 15 minutes, to prevent burned cake bottoms.

To prevent soggy-bottom pie crusts, brush unbaked crust with beaten egg whites before filling.

For the highest meringue, add a pinch of baking powder to room temperature egg whites before beating.

Whipped cream made ahead of time won't separate, if you add ¼ teaspoon of dissolved unflavoured gelatin per cup of cream.

A tablespoon of cornstarch added to a cake just before putting it into the pan, makes it lighter and less likely to fall.

Cooking Hints

A few drops of lemon juice added to water in which rice is to be cooked, keeps rice fluffy, and prevents it from sticking together.

Use dental floss to truss turkey or chicken, as it is strong and does not burn.

Baking fish on a bed of chopped onion, celery and parsley, adds flavour and prevents fish from sticking to the bottom of the pan.

To prevent boilovers when cooking noodles, rice or spaghetti, add a pat of butter or a few teaspoons of vegetable oil to water.

Adding a pinch of soda when making gravy cuts the grease and keeps it from floating on top.

Raw chicken is easiest to cut up when it is slightly frozen — just to the point of stiffening.

Retain the juices in a roast by not carving the meat for 15 minutes after taking it from the oven. This allows the juices to settle back in the meat rather than spurting out onto the carving board.

Prevent butter from burning when sauteing, by adding a small amount of oil. Butter alone burns easily, but the combination of the two does not.

The easiest and best deep-frying batter results from mixing equal quantities of flour and beer. Good for any food, it provides a thin, light coating that fries crisp without absorbing excess fat.

Just-cooked pasta should be rinsed under hot water, rather than cold water. It washes off the excess starch and keeps the pasta hot at the same time.

To keep hot fat from splattering, sprinkle a little salt or flour in the pan before frying.

Vegetables & Fruits

Cook broccoli stems as quickly as the flowers by making a one-inch x-like incision from the bottom up on the stems. This allows the heat to penetrate and the stems to cook faster.

To help keep cauliflower white, add a little milk to the water in which it is cooked.

For extra-crisp French fried potatoes, peel and slice the potatoes and soak the pieces in ice-cold water for about half an hour. Drain and dry potatoes thoroughly; then fry as usual.

Wilted vegetables can be freshened by soaking one hour in a mixture of cold water and the juice of one lemon (or a few tablespoons of vinegar).

To prevent beets from fading, cook them whole with 2 inches of stem left on.

To get more juice from citrus fruits, heat the lemons, oranges or grapefruit in the oven, or immerse in very hot water for about five minutes.

Salads

Don't add salt to salad until just before serving, as this wilts and toughens lettuce.

To prevent soggy salads, place an inverted saucer in the bottom of the salad bowl. The excess liquid drains off under the saucer and salad stays crisp.

Cheese

Store cottage cheese upside down.

To cut cheese, use a warm or dull knife.

Before grating cheese, oil the grater so that the cheese will come off more easily.

Index

Almonds
Almond Chicken 98

Appetizers
Cold:
Cheese Walnut Log 22
Christmas Kutia 27
Pickled Shrimp and Mushrooms 21
Shrimp Cheese Ball 22
Shrimp, Ham or Mushroom Hors D'Oeurves 20
Smoked Salmon Spread 19

Hot:
Bacon Wrapped Water Chestnuts 23
Cheese Snack 28
Hot Meat and Cheese Puffs 21
Olive 'n' Cheese Rolls 19

Apples
Apple Cheese Pizza 166
Apple Cinnamon Puffs 186
Apple Pancakes 215
Applesauce Bread 201
Applesauce Muffins 196
Bavarian Apple Torte 173
Carrot Pudding 170
Cheese Crumble Pie 168
Danish Apple Bars 182
Dutch Apple Streusel Coffee Cake 198
French Apple Pie 162
German Strudel 174
Green Tomato Mincemeat 235
Molded Waldorf Salad 48
Zucchini and Apple Chutney 230

Apricots
Apricot and Raisin Quickbread 195

Bananas
Banana Bread 202

Banana Crunch Cake	147
Banana Flambe	146
Banana Slice	176
Banana Slush	11
Banana Split Dessert	181
Blueberry Banana Pie	161
Fruit Marshmallow Salad	30
Jellied Salad	45
Trifle	179

Bars

Cake Bars

Fudgy Oatmeal Brownies	187
Kuehen	175
Tweedies	185

Fruit — Filled:

Danish Apple Bars	182
Pineapple Slices	183

Sweet:

Buttertart Squares	137
Chocolate Mint Bars	142
Hello Dollies	187
Peanut Butter Slice	184
Ricketty Uncles	183
Sweet Marie Bars	184

Batter

Beer Batter for Fondue	227

Beans

Bean Salad	34
Cashew Rice and Beans	83
Chililess Chili	107
Cowboy Bean Casserole	86
Dilled Bean Pickles	237
Old Fashioned Boston Baked Beans	63

Beef

Ground:

Bierrocks	101
Buckwheat Cabbage Rolls	132
Cabbage Rolls	130
Chililess Chili	107

Deluxe Meat Loaf	124
Ground Beef Casserole	74
Hawaiian Hamburgers	109
Heavenly Hash Casserole	86
Hot Meat and Cheese Puffs	21
Lasagne	128
Manicotti	73
Meatball Stroganoff	134
Mexicali Lasagna	129
Mini Meat Pies	104
Oriental Beef Casserole	84
Souper Skillet Pasta	75
Spanish Noodles	72
Stir Fried Beef and Zucchini	115
Stuffed Green Peppers	108
Super Spaghetti and Meat Balls	100
Witches Brew	77

Steak:
Always Tender Steak in Foil	113
Beef Kabobs	126
Rouladen	114
Boeuf Bourguignonne	112
Pepper Steak	123
Rolled Stuffed Flank Steak	131
Stir Fry Beef and Broccoli	124
Stir Fried Beef and Zucchini	115
Swiss Steak	118

Stewing:
Chop Suey	103
Hearty Beef and Vegetable Soup	49
Oven Beef Stew	116

Beets

Beet and Carrot Cake	153
Beet Horseradish Relish	232
Beet Jelly	231
Beet Relish	233
Harvard Beets	62
Pickled Beets	235
Ukranian Borsch	51

Beverages

Cold:
Banana Slush	11

247

Beer Punch	10
Carob Drink	14
Easy Egg Nog	16
Festive Punch	16
Frozen Dacquiri	12
Hawaiian Slush	12
Honey Bunch Punch	13
Summer Joy Punch	11
Wedding Punch	10

Hot:

Eggnog Brasilia	15
Russian Tea	14
Wassail	15
Winter Warmers	13

Biscuits

Baking Powder Biscuits	220
Scottish Tea Scones	221
Welsh Tea Cakes	221

Blueberries

Blueberry Banana Pie	161
Blueberry Slump	139

Bratwurst

Hot German Potato Salad	81

Bread

Breakfast Casserole	74
Cottage Cheese Cake	145
Dutch Brunch	77
Old Fashioned Bread Pudding	169

Breads

Basic:

Cheddar Bread	213
Homemade Bread	209

Cereal:

Bishop's Bread	201
Grain Bread	205
Nuts and Seeds Bread	200

Fruit:

Applesauce Bread	201

Apricot and Raisin Quickbread 195
Banana Bread 202
Norwegian Bread 200

Special Occasion:
Swiss Christmas Bread 207

Vegetable:
Corn Bread 213
French Onion Bread 203
Zucchini Bread 204

Broccoli

Almond Chicken 98
Broccoli Onion Deluxe 60
Broccoli Salad 37
Marinated Salad 30
Stir Fry Beef and Broccoli 124

Buns

Basic:
Air Buns 211
Overnight Buns 210
Quick Buns 210

Variety:
Cinnamon Buns 212
Hot Cross Buns 208
Trinidadian Pita 204

Cabbage

Beet Horseradish Relish 232
Buckwheat Cabbage Rolls 132
Cabbage Rolls 130
14 Day Coleslaw 31
Molded Coleslaw 40
Sweet and Sour Red Cabbage 58
Ukranian Borsch 51
White Borsch 51

Cake

Christmas:
Icelandic Christmas Cake 146
Light Christmas Cake 144

Coffee Cakes:
Dutch Apple Streusel Coffee Cake 198
Poppy Seed Coffee Cake 199

Crumb and Filled:
Banana Crunch Cake 147
Bavarian Apple Torte 173
Coconut Butterscotch Cake. 158
Cottage Cheese Cake 145
Jelly Roll. 188
Streusel Crumb Cake 148
Tweedies 185

Layer:
Grasshopper Cake 149
Shortbread Layer Cake 152

Loaf:
Chocolate Date Cake 150
Kahlua Loaf Cake. 198
Mediwnyk 158

Sponge:
Chocolate Cherry Swirl Cake. 141
Chocolate Chiffon Cake 136
Luscious Orange Sponge Cake. 143
Mabel's Harvey Wallbanger Cake. 150

Staple:
Beet and Carrot Cake 153
Boiled Raisin Cake 144
Katorshnik 214
Tomato Soup Cake 154

Candy

Chocolate Coconut Candies 140
Health Fudge 139

Carrots

Beet and Carrot Cake. 153
Carrot and Mushroom Stir Fry 59
Carrot and Spinach. 57
Carrot Pudding. 170
Cheese Soup 54
14 Day Coleslaw 31
Hearty Beef and Vegetable Soup. 49
Marinated Carrot Salad 33
Minestrone Soup 52

Sunshine Carrots 61
Sweet Cream Carrot Salad 48
Vegetable Relish Maranata 233

Casserole

Beef:
Ground Beef Casserole 74
Heavenly Hash Casserole 86
Manicotti 73
Oriental Beef Casserole 84
Souper Skillet Pasta 75
Spanish Noodles 72
Witches Brew 77

Eggs:
Basic Souffle 85
Dutch Brunch 77
Foamy Omelet 75
Gerrie's Quiche 76

Pork:
Breakfast Casserole 74
Cowboy Bean Casserole 86
Sausage Rich Luncheon Dish 82
Scallopped Sausage and Potatoes 82

Poultry:
Chicken Chow Bake 76
Chicken or Turkey Pineapple Casserole 78

Rice:
Brown Rice and Cheese 89

Vegetable:
Cashew Rice and Beans 83
Eggplant Casserole 84
Hot German Potato Salad 81
Imperial Potato Puff 80
Olive and Mushroom Casserole 89
Potatoes Au Gratin Casserole 80
Zucchini Paramigiana 79

Cauliflower

Almond Chicken 98
Antipasto 234
Marinated Salad 30
Vegetable Chowder 52
Vegetable Relish Maranata 233

Celery
- Cheese Soup 54
- Minestrone Soup 52

Cheese

Cottage:
- Cottage Cheese Cake 145
- Cottage Cheese Salad 43
- Lasagne 128
- Lyszniki 216
- Manicotti 73
- Perogies 65

Hard:
- Apple Cheese Pizza 166
- Brown Rice and Cheese Casserole 89
- Cheddar Bread 213
- Cheese Cookies 178
- Cheese Crumble Pie 168
- Cheese Snack 28
- Cheese Soup 54
- Dutch Brunch 77
- Hot Meat and Cheese Puffs 21
- Olive 'n' Cheese Rolls 19
- Pineapple Cheese Salad 43
- Pizza Bun Mix 226
- Potatoes Au Gratin Casserole 80

Soft:
- Bavarian Apple Torte 173
- Broccoli Onion Deluxe 173
- Cheese Walnut Log 22
- Cherry Cheesecake 151
- Chicken Mozzarella 102
- Chili Con Queso Dip 25
- Chocolate Dessert 166
- Crab Dip 23
- Eggplant Casserole 84
- Hors D'Oeurves 20
- Imperial Potato Puff 80
- Lasagne 128
- Layered Cherry Cheese Mold 46
- Mexicali Lasagna 129
- Pineapple Chocolate Cheesecake 159
- Shrimp Cheese Ball 22
- Shrimp Dip 25

Smoked Salmon Spread 19
Velvet Salad 44

Chillies

Barbequed Spareribs 116
Chili Con Queso Dip 25
Sopa De Elate 50

Cherries

Cherry Cheesecake 151
Cherry Cho Cho 168
Cherry Loaf. 206
Chocolate Cherry Swirl Cake. 141
Layered Cherry Cheese Mold. 46

Coffee

Cafe au Lait Whipped Frosting 136
Coffee Tortoni 165
Winter Warmers. 13

Cookies

Drop:
Bachelor Buttons 180
Butterscotch Jumbles 178
Cheese Cookies 178
Chocolate Raisin Clusters 140
Coconut Date Balls. 141
Oh So Good Cookies 176

Rolled:
Dutch Cookies 157
Ginger Sparklers 177
Graham Wafers 164
Pfeffernusse. 172
Sand Cookies 177

Corn

Heavenly Hash Casserole 86
Sopa De Elate 50

Cranberries

Cranberry Pie 161

Crepes

- Chicken Filled Crepes 96
- Crepes Suzette 219
- Lyszniki 216

Cucumbers

- Bread and Butter Pickles 236
- Cucumber Salad 34
- Dill Pickles 237
- Sweet Dill Pickles 238

Desserts

Chilled Slice:
- Banana Split Dessert 181
- Cherry Cheesecake 151
- Cherry Cho Cho 168
- Chocolate Dessert 166
- Chocolate Mint Bars 142
- Coffee Tortoni 165
- Pineapple Chocolate Cheesecake 159
- Pumpkin Ice Cream Squares 180
- Trifle 179

Hot Cake:
- Apple Cheese Pizza 166
- Apple Cinnamon Puffs 186
- Banana Flambe 146
- Blueberry Slump 139
- German Strudel 174
- Plum Crumb Dessert 171

Dips

- Bacon Dip 'n' Dunk 26
- Chili Con Queso Dip 25
- Crab Dip 24
- Curry Dip 23
- Fresh Fruit Dip 26
- Shrimp Dip 25
- Vegetable Dip 24

Dumplings

- Lamb Stew with Dumplings 105

Eggs

Basic Souffle	85
Breakfast Casserole	74
Chocolate Chiffon Cake	136
Dutch Brunch	77
Easy Egg Nog	16
Eggnog Brasilia	15
Foamy Omelet	75
Gerrie's Quiche	76
Jelly Roll	188
Pickled Eggs	234

Ethnic

Bierrocks	101
Chicken Chow Bake	76
Diced Pork and Cashews	120
Chinese Pork Tenderloin	119
Chop Suey	103
Christmas Kutia	27
Dutch Brunch	77
French Canadian Tourtiere	125
German Strudel	174
Holushkia	130
Hot German Potato Salad	81
Mexicali Lasagna	129
Mexican Corn Soup	50
Nachinka Corn Meal Dressing	214
Pfeffernusse	172
Perogies	65
Polynesian Chicken and Peaches	108
Pyrohy	64
Rouladen	114
Schnitzel	127
Trinidadian Pita	204
Ukranian Borsch	51

Grain

Bran:

Best Bran Muffins	197
Bran Muffins	192
Grain Bread	205

Buckwheat:

Buckwheat Cabbage Rolls	132

Cornmeal:
Corn Bread 213
Hush Puppies 220
Lemon Baked Fish Fillets 106
Nachinka Corn Meal Dressing 214

Rolled Oats:
Bishop's Bread 201
Fudgy Oatmeal Brownies 187
Oat Muffins 196
Oh So Good Cookies 176
Ricketty Uncles 183
Sand Cookies 177

Wheat:
Christmas Kutia 27

Wheat Germ:
Grain Bread 205
Wheat Germ Muffins 194

Ice Cream
Pumpkin Ice Cream Squares 180
Ice Cream Festive Punch 16
Ice Salad 41

Icing
Cooked:
Cafe au Lait Whipped Frosting 136
Soft Icing 173

Uncooked:
Bakery Shop Icing 152
Uncooked Marshmallow Frosting 154

Jam
Beet Jelly 231
Heavenly Jam 230
Rhubarb Jam 229
Zucchini and Apple Chutney 230

Juice
Banana Slush 11
Festive Punch 16
Frozen Dacquiri 12
Hawaiian Slush 12

Honey Bunch Punch	13
Russian Tea	14
Wassail	15
Wedding Punch	10

Lamb
Lamb Stew with Dumplings	105

Lentils
Lentil Stew	68

Lettuce
Layered Salad	38

Loaf
Fruit:
Applesauce Bread	20
Apricot and Raisin Quickbread	195
Banana Bread	202
Cherry Loaf	206
Date and Nut Loaf	206
Kahlua Loaf Cake	198

Grain:
Bishop's Bread	201

Spice:
Cinnamon Loaf	202

Vegetable:
Zucchini Bread	204

Meat Accompaniment
Nachinka Corn Meal Dressing	214
Wild Rice Stuffing	63
Yorkshire Pudding	215

Microwave Methods
Bacon Wrapped Water Chestnuts	23
Chicken Mozzarella	102
Sausage Rice Luncheon Dish	82
Spanish Noodles	72

Milk
Carob Drink	14

Easy Egg Nog, ... 16
Eggnog Brasilia 15

Milk Products

Condensed Milk:
Hello Dollies 187
Salad Dressing 42

Sour Cream:
Ambrosia 40
Chicken Paprika 98
Fresh Fruit Dip 26
Meatball Stroganoff 134
Potatoes Au Gratin Casserole 80
Schnitzel 127
Shrimp Elegante 92
Sour Cream Raisin Pie 162
Super Mushroom Soup 50
Vegetable Dip 24

Whipped Cream:
Cottage Cheese Salad 43
Fruit Marshmallow Salad 30
Fruit Salad 41
Pineapple Cheese Salad 43
Sweet Cream Carrot Salad 48
Molded Waldorf Salad 48

Yogurt:
Bacon Dip 'n' Dunk 26
Curry Dip 24

Muffins

Cereal:
Best Bran Muffins 197
Bran Muffins 192
Oat Muffins 196
Wheat Germ Muffins 194

Fruit:
Applesauce Muffins 196
Date and Orange Muffins 192
Pumpkin Muffins 193

Spice:
Cinnamon Muffins 194

Mushrooms

Bacon Fried Rice 67
Beef Kabobs 126
Broccoli Salad 37
Carrot and Mushroom Stir Fry 59
Chicken Paprika 98
Mushroom Hors D'Oeurves 20
Olive and Mushroom Casserole 89
Stuffed Tomatoes 60
Super Mushroom Soup 50

Olives

Olive 'n' Cheese Rolls 19
Olive and Mushroom Casserole 89

Onions

Beef Kabobs 126
Cheese Soup 54
Chili Sauce 227
French Onion Bread 203
French Onion Soup 53

Oranges

Ambrosia 40
Duckling A L'Orange 110
Luscious Orange Sponge Cake 143
Orange Butter Crescents 222
Trifle 179

Pancakes

Basic:
Apple Pancakes 215
Potato Pancakes 218

Filled:
Crepes Suzette 219
Lyszniki 216

Variety:
Bannock 216
Hush Puppies 220
Waffles 218

Pasta

Lasagna:
Lasagne 128
Mexicali Lasagna 129

Macaroni:
Heavenly Hash Casserole 86
Macaroni Salad 30
Meatball Stroganoff 134
Souper Skillet Pasta 75
Spanish Noodles 72

Manicotti:
Manicotti 73

Spaghetti:
Super Spaghetti and Meatballs 100

Pastry

Flaky Pastry 160
Perfect Pie Crust 157

Peaches

Heavenly Jam 230
Peach Crumbly Crust Pie 188
Polynesian Chicken and Peaches 108

Pears

Fruit Salad 41
Heavenly Jam 230

Peppers

Beef Kabobs 126
Chinese Pork Tenderloin 119
Layered Salad 38
Marinated Carrot Salad 33
Oriental Beef Casserole 84
Pepper Steak 123
Rice Stuffed Green Peppers 62
Stuffed Green Peppers 108

Perogies

Lazy Man or Do' Boy Perogies 66
Perogies 65
Pyrohy 64

Pickles

Dill
Dilled Bean ... 237
Dill Pickles ... 237

Sweet:
Bread and Butter Pickles ... 236
Pickled Beets ... 235
Pickled Eggs ... 234
Sweet Dill Pickles ... 238

Pies

Cream:
Grasshopper Pie ... 160
Impossible Pie ... 167
Mud Pie ... 163

Fruit:
Banana Slice ... 176
Blueberry Banana Pie ... 161
Cheese Crumble Pie ... 168
Cranberry Pie ... 161
French Apple Pie ... 162
Peach Crumbly Crust Pie ... 188
Sour Cream Raisin Pie ... 162

Pineapple

Banana Split Dessert ... 181
Chicken Chow Bake ... 76
Cottage Cheese Salad ... 43
Fruit Salad ... 41
Hawaiian Hamburgers ... 109
Ice Salad ... 41
Jellied Salad ... 45
Pineapple Cheese Salad ... 43
Pineapple Chocolate Cheesecake ... 159
Pineapple Sesame Chicken ... 99
Pineapple Slices ... 183
Rhubarb Jam ... 223
Squash with Pineapple ... 59
Sweet Cream Carrot Salad ... 48
Sweet and Sour Pork Chops ... 130
Velvet Salad ... 44

Plums
  Plum Crumb Dessert 171

Popcorn
  Chemist's Christmas Concoction 138

Pork
  Bacon:
  Bacon Dip 'n' Dunk 26
  Bacon Fried Rice 66
  Bacon Wrapped Water Chestnuts 23
  Boeuf Bourguignonne 112
  Cabbage Rolls (Holushkia) 130
  Chililess Chili 107
  Deluxe Meat Loaf 124
  Gerrie's Quiche 76
  Hot German Potato Salad 81
  New England Clam Chowder 54
  Old Fashion Boston Baked Beans 63
  Rouladen 114
  Savory Zucchini 56
  Sweet and Sour Red Cabbage 58

  Chops:
  Barbecued Pork Chops 113
  Schnitzel 127
  Sweet and Sour Pork Chops 130

  Ground:
  Cabbage Rolls 130
  Deluxe Meat Loaf 124
  French Canadian Tourtiere 125
  Super Spaghetti and Meatballs 100

  Ham:
  Chicken Mozzarella 102
  Cowboy Bean Casserole 86
  Glazed Ham 117
  Ham Hors D'Oeurves 20

  Sausage:
  Breakfast Casserole 74
  Sausage Rice Luncheon Dish 82
  Scallopped Sausage and Potatoes 82

  Spareribs:
  Baked Stuffed Spareribs 116

Barbecued Spareribs 133
Grandma's Sweet Ribs.. 126
Honey and Garlic Ribs... 111
Ukranian Borsch 51

Tenderloin:
Chinese Pork Tenderloin 119
Chop Suey.. 103
Diced Pork and Cashews 120

Potato

Carrot Pudding... 170
Chocolate Coconut Candies 140
French Canadian Tourtiere 125
Hearty Beef and Vegetable Soup................................ 49
Hot German Potato Salad 81
Imperial Potato Puff 80
Katorshnik 214
Lazy-Man or Do' Boy Perogies 66
Perogies 65
Picnic Potato Salad 44
Potatoes Au Gratin Casserole 80
Potato Pancakes... 218
Pyrohy 64
Scallopped Sausage and Potatoes 82
Vegetable Chowder 52

Poultry

Chicken:
Almond Chicken.. 98
Chicken Cacciatore.. 114
Chicken Chop Suey... 103
Chicken Chow Bake 76
Chicken Filled Crepes... 96
Chicken Fried Rice.. 118
Chicken Mozzarella.. 102
Chicken Paprika... 98
Cool Chicken Salad.. 32
Oven Barbequed Chicken.. 95
Polynesian Chicken and Peaches................................ 108
Scrumptious Summer Salad 42
Sesame Chicken 99

Duck:
Duckling A L'Orange... 110

Turkey:
Turkey Pineapple Casserole 78

Pudding
Carrot Pudding. 170
Old Fashioned Bread Pudding. 169
Tapioca Pudding 169

Pumpkin
Pumpkin Ice Cream Squares 180
Pumpkin Muffins. 193

Quiche
Gerrie's Quiche 76

Relish
Antipasto 234
Beet Horseradish Relish 232
Beet Relish 233
Fresh Onion Cucumber Relish. 232
Green Tomato Mincemeat 235
Vegetable Relish Maranata 233

Rice
Bacon Fried Rice 67
Brown Rice and Cheese Casserole 89
Cabbage Rolls (Holushkia). 130
Cashew Rice and Beans 83
Chicken Fried Rice 118
Chicken or Turkey Pineapple Casserole 78
Fruit Marshmallow Salad 30
Ground Beef Casserole. 74
Rice Italienne 66
Stuffed Green Peppers. 108
Sausage Rice Luncheon Dish 82
Shrimp Elegante. 92
Tomato and Rice Soup 49
Tuna Puff 93
Wild Rice Stuffing 63
Witches Brew 77

Rhubarb
Rhubarb Jam 229

Rhubarb Sherbet 164

Rolls
Orange Butter Crescents 222
Scuffles 217

Salads
Fruit:
Ambrosia 40
Fruit Marshmallow Salad 30
Fruit Salad 41
Watergate Salad 38

Molded:
Blushing Shrimp Salad 39
Cottage Cheese Salad 43
Cucumber Salad 34
Ice Salad 41
Jellied Salad 45
Layered Cherry Cheese Mold 46
Molded Coleslaw 40
Molded Waldorf Salad 48
Pineapple Cheese Salad 43
Sweet Cream Carrot Salad 48
Scrumptious Summer Salad 42
Two Tone Christmas Jellied Salad 47
Velvet Salad 44

Vegetable
Bean Salad 34
Broccoli Salad 37
Cool Chicken Salad 32
14 Day Coleslaw 31
Layered Salad 38
Macaroni Salad 30
Marinated Carrot Salad 33
Marinated Salad 39
Picnic Potato Salad 44
Sauerkraut Salad 32
Zucchini Salad 37

Salad Dressing 42

Sauces
Dessert:
Butterscotch Cream Sauce 229

265

Chocolate Fudge Sauce 228
Fish:
Tartar Sauce 226
Tomato:
Chili Sauce 227
Pizza Bun Mix 226
Tomato Ketchup. 228

Seafood

Crab:
Crab Dip 23
Scrumptious Summer Salad 42
Clams:
New England Clam Chowder 54
Fish:
Lemon Baked Fish Fillets 106
Oriental Perch Fillets 107
Salmon:
Salmon Cups 97
Scrumptious Summer Salad 42
Smoked Salmon Spread 19
Scallops:
Seafood Appetizers 94
Shrimp:
Antipasto 234
Blushing Shrimp Salad 39
Scrumptious Summer Salad 42
Seafood Appetizers 94
Shrimp Cheese Ball 22
Shrimp Creole 92
Shrimp Dip 25
Shrimp Elegante 92
Shrimp Hors D'Oeurves 20
Macaroni Salad 30
Pickled Shrimp and Mushrooms, ... 21
Tuna:
Scrumptious Summer Salad 42
Tuna Cups 97
Tuna Puff 93
Oysters:
Oyster Stew 95
Shrimp Cheese Ball 22

Seeds

Poppy:
Christmas Kutia 27
German Strudel 174
Nuts and Seeds Bread 200
Poppy Seed Coffee Cake 199

Sesame:
Eggplant Casserole 84
Health Fudge 139
Nuts and Seeds Bread 200

Sunflower:
Health Fudge 139
Toasted Granola 28

Sherbet

Festive Punch 16
Rhubarb Sherbet 164

Soup

Clear:
French Onion 53
Hearty Beef and Vegetable 49
Minestrone Soup 52

Cream:
Cheese Soup 54
New England Clam Chowder 54
Sopa De Elate (Mexican Corn Soup) 50
Super Mushroom 50
Tomato and Rice 49
Ukranian Borsch 51
Vegetable Chowder 52
White Borsch 51

Spinach

Carrots and Spinach 57
Lasagne 128

Squash

Squash With Pineapple 59

Stew

Lamb Stew with Dumplings 105

Lentil Stew	68
Oven Beef Stew	116
Oyster Stew	95
Tomato Venison Stew	102

Strawberries
Beer Punch	10
Summer Joy Punch	11

Syrup
Pancake Syrup	231

Taco Chips
Mexicali Lasagna	129

Tapioca
Tapioca Pudding	169

Tarts
Butter Tarts	186

Tea
Winter Warmers	13

Tomato
Beef Kabobs	126
Chili Con Queso Dip	25
Chili Sauce	227
Green Tomato Mincemeat	235
Minestrone Soup	52
Pizza Bun Mix	226
Stuffed Tomatoes	60
Tomato Ketchup	228
Tomato Soup Cake	154
Vegetable Chowder	52
Zucchini Parmigiana	79

Tomato Juice
Blushing Shrimp Salad	39
Tomato and Rice Soup	49

Venison
Tomato Venison Stew 102

Zucchini
Cool Chicken Salad... 32
Savory Zucchini 56
Stir-Fried Beef and Zucchini 115
Zucchini and Apple Chutney 230
Zucchini Bread 204
Zucchini Creole 67
Zucchini Parmigiana 79
Zucchini Salad 37
Zucchini Scallop 56

Share *Wheatland Bounty* with a friend

Order *Wheatland Bounty* at $15.95 per book plus $3.50 (total order) for postage and handling.

Number of books _____ x $15.95 = $ _____
Postage and handling _____ = $ ___3.50___
Subtotal _____ = $ _____
In Canada add 7% GST OR 15% HST where applicable _____ = $ _____
Total enclosed _____ = $ _____

U.S. and international orders payable in U.S. funds./Price is subject to change.

NAME _____
STREET _____
CITY _____ PROV./STATE _____
COUNTRY _____ POSTAL CODE/ZIP _____

Please make cheque or money order payable to:
**S.S.M.L.T.
P.O. Box 3837
Regina, Saskatchewan,
Canada S4P 3R8**

Please allow 3-4 weeks for delivery.

Share *Wheatland Bounty* with a friend

Order *Wheatland Bounty* at $15.95 per book plus $3.50 (total order) for postage and handling.

Number of books _____ x $15.95 = $ _____
Postage and handling _____ = $ ___3.50___
Subtotal _____ = $ _____
In Canada add 7% GST OR 15% HST where applicable _____ = $ _____
Total enclosed _____ = $ _____

U.S. and international orders payable in U.S. funds./Price is subject to change.

NAME _____
STREET _____
CITY _____ PROV./STATE _____
COUNTRY _____ POSTAL CODE/ZIP _____

Please make cheque or money order payable to:
**S.S.M.L.T.
P.O. Box 3837
Regina, Saskatchewan,
Canada S4P 3R8**

Please allow 3-4 weeks for delivery.